JEAN GARRIGUE

JEAN GARRIGUE

A Poetics of Plenitude

Lee Upton

Rutherford ● Madison ● Teaneck
Fairleigh Dickinson University Press
London and Toronto: Associated University Presses

Associated University Presses
440 Forsgate Drive
Cranbury, NJ 08512

Associated University Presses
25 Sicilian Avenue
London WC1A 2QH, England

Associated University Presses
P.O. Box 488, Port Credit
Mississauga, Ontario
Canada L5G 4M2

The paper used in this publication meets the requirements
of the American National Standard for Permanence of Paper
for Printed Library Materials Z39.48-1984.

Library of Congress Cataloging-in-Publication Data

Upton, Lee, 1953–
  Jean Garrigue : a poetics of plenitude / Lee Upton.
    p.   cm.
  Includes index.
  ISBN 0-8386-3397-8 (alk. paper)
  1. Garrigue, Jean. 1912–1972—Criticism and interpretation.
I. Title.
PS3513.A7217Z9   1991
811'.54—dc20   89-46416
                                                   CIP

PRINTED IN THE UNITED STATES OF AMERICA

CONTENTS

ACKNOWLEDGMENTS

I am grateful to my colleagues at Lafayette College for their kind encouragement. Acknowledgment is also due early readers of this study who offered valuable insights: Susan Strehle, Sandra Cypess, Gayle Whittier—and, most especially, Mary Lynn Broe. I am indebted to Marjorie Garrigue Smith for providing me with important information about her sister. The executors Leslie Katz and Aileen Ward have been remarkably generous in numerous conversations and letters. I wish to thank them for their support of this project. Jane Mayhall's criticism of Jean Carrigue prompted me to engage in my own explorations, and her knowledge of Jean Garrigue's poetry, like that of the executors, has been inspiring. Unpublished materials from the Jean Garrigue archive are used with permission from the estate and the Albert A. Berg Collection of the New York Public Library, Astor, Lenox, and Tilden Foundations. Jean Garrigue's poems are reprinted with permission of the estate. Finally, I wish to thank my husband, Eric Ziolkowski, who unfailingly and daily earns my gratitude.

Portions of chapter 1, in altered form, appeared in *Soundings: An Interdisciplinary Journal*. Portions of chapter 4, in altered form, appeared in the *Denver Quarterly*.

ABBREVIATIONS

JEAN GARRIGUE

INTRODUCTION

Jean Garrigue's is an elaborate, occasionally theatrical poetry. Like the actress she wrote of in her posthumously published collection, this poet must always be "acting the whole part out" (SFA, 9) depicting plenitudinous selfhood. As one of the more prominent American women poets at midcentury, Garrigue (1912–72) was strikingly independent, characterized by Theodore Roethke as "trust[ing] her sensibility more completely than any other poet" with whom he was acquainted.[1] She published seven books of poems, a novella, a collection of prose poems, and many critical reviews and short stories. Among the poets with whom she was closely associated were May Swenson and Stanley Kunitz. She was the recipient of grants and awards from the Guggenheim Foundation, the National Institute of Arts and Letters, and the Rockefeller Foundation. As poetry editor of the *New Leader* from 1965 to 1971 she reviewed her contemporaries with insight and goodwill in meticulous prose. She edited a collection of love poems and an early anthology of translations by American poets. Her 1964 volume, *Country Without Maps*, received a nomination for the National Book Award. Her final volume, the culmination of a distinguished and exacting career, appeared in 1973, a year after Garrigue's death of Hodgkin's disease.

Many of Garrigue's contemporaries praised her work highly. Harvey Shapiro has written: "Her way with language was Mozartean, breathtaking in its ability to ring change after change on a theme, Mozartean bursts of language, never leaving the subject, enabling the eye to see, clearly and more clearly, while delighting the ear with sound."[2] To Robert Lowell, Garrigue was "a brilliant poet" whose work reveals "a kind of Book of Hours simplicity."[3] To Adrienne Rich, Garrigue's poem "After Reading *The Country of the Pointed Firs*" is "as good or better than most of Frost."[4] To Stephen Stepanchev, her "lyricism and technical brilliance . . . make her visions persuasive and distinctive."[5] Babette Deutsch in *Poetry in Our Time* calls Garrigue an "intense, profound, and subtle poet."[6] Laurence Lieberman writes that "there are rewards to be secured in reading [Garrigue's] best poems of a kind that can be found in no other body of work."[7] More recently, in a 1982 Hofstra symposium such poets as May Swenson, Stanley Kunitz, and Richard Eberhart gathered to discuss Garrigue's poetry. Kunitz called Garrigue "a wildly gifted poet . . . whose art took the road of excess that leads to the palace of wisdom." Garrigue was, Kunitz said, "our one lyric poet who made ecstasy her home."[8]

Certain of Garrigue's aesthetic values are clear even to the reader first encountering her work. For one thing, "more is more." In an autobiographical sketch Garrigue would write, "I prefer elaborate structures to functional slick ones."[9] She favors anticlimax and a stylistic complexity that borrows some of the textures of metaphysical verse. She extends upon focal images, creating structures of magnitude. She developed her own poetic landscape and wrote frequently of subterranean opportunity within the limits of circumstance. She regretted the loss of any contemporary sense of godhead, and yet, conversely, she affronted traditional godhead. Imaginative power was for her a form of dramatic self-spending; in turn, she traced out the deadening consequences of silence and isolation.

"Every line in a poem is an autobiography,"[10] Garrigue was to insist. If her poems suggest that she was a laureate of restlessness, her life reflects a similar commitment to flux. The daughter of a postal inspector who had himself written short stories, Garrigue's independence was manifested early. She was born in Evansville, Indiana on 8 December 1912 under the name Gertrude Louise Garrigus, the lateborn daughter of Allan Colfax, aged forty-four, and Gertrude (Heath) Garrigus, thirty-nine. "Dim Hugenot ancestors on one side—English mixed with Scotch on the other."[11] Her sister Marjorie, later to become a concert pianist, was already eleven, her brother Ross, then eighteen, was to become a newspaper editor. As her sister Marjorie puts it, Garrigue was always to "rebel against conventions and even common-sense rules of health. She had to feel she had absolute freedom. . . ."[12] At fourteen she "discovered" Shelley, Keats, and the Imagists, "especially H.D."[13]

She attended Butler College in Indianapolis before transferring to the University of Chicago, rooming with the novelist Marguerite Young. In 1937, after graduation, she returned to Indiana to work on a newspaper. Within four years she moved to Greenwich Village, changed her name (a patriotic grandfather had altered the surname from the original Garrigues to the more

"American-sounding" Garrigus) and took up the poetry she had begun as a schoolgirl, feeling at last "delivered" and "in possession of a tongue."[14]

In 1943 Garrigue received a master of fine arts in the writing program at the University of Iowa. After graduation she returned to New York where she earned her living through freelance writing and editing before teaching at a variety of institutions, including Bard College, Queens College, the New School for Social Research, the University of Connecticut, and Smith College. She was to receive prestigious awards and grants, among them Rockefeller and Hudson Review fellowships, the Emily Clark Balch Prize from the *Virginia Quarterly Review*, the Longview Award, the Melville Cane Award, and in 1970 an honorary doctorate from Skidmore College. After her death in 1972, the critical climate that at last began to take increased notice of women poets would favor those whose language was more direct and more readily available to critical theory. Within the traditional canon, Marianne Moore and Elizabeth Bishop were praised for what superficially seemed to be objectivity and distance, while poets who were directly and outspokenly concerned with women's issues captured the attention of most feminist critics. Although her battle against women's silence runs throughout much of her work, paradoxically Garrigue was often deliberately nonhistorical, refusing to focus social forces. In the same year that "no more masks" became a rallying cry and the title of an important anthology of women's poetry, Garrigue's posthumous volume appeared in which the poet self-consciously investigates, celebrates, and exploits the power of masking. Elaborate, double-tongued, highly stylized, this poet praised women and women's lives and fashioned an actress figure with enormous appetitive power. And yet her facility with a range of styles, her elevated rhetoric, her reliance on some aspects of traditional prosody, her very complexity of language and perspective frustrate critical reception. Frequently reviewers of the posthumous volume took a curatorial approach. Her speakers, often women of intense, "unmanageable" feeling, caused discomfort among some critics while eliciting cryptic, near-erotic praise from others and less than subtle misogyny from a minority.

Garrigue's poems were introduced in the *Kenyon Review* in the fall of 1941 along with those of such other young poets as John Ciardi, Reed Whittemore, Howard Nemerov, and Howard Moss. Three years later her poems were included in a New Directions volume of five young poets. Her collection within the volume,

Thirty-Six Poems and a Few Songs, develops the theme of divi-
sions within the self, between lovers, and between mind and
nature. It is an ambitious first collection and announces its ambitions, moving from loss of a lover-muse to a sense of curative
experience. Of the poets introduced by New Directions in 1944—
Alejandro Carrion, John Frederick Nims, Eve Merriam, and a
Tennessee Williams that Randall Jarrell not altogether jokingly
regarded as a "hoax"—Garrigue was described repeatedly by
reviewers as the most substantial. To Jarrell she was "much the
best" of the group, her poems exhibiting "the guaranteeing and
personal queerness of a diary."[15]

Garrigue's second book, *The Ego and the Centaur* (1947), is
even more ambitious than her first, and yet it is perhaps the most
disappointing of her collections. The volume is more varied than
its predecessor. Too often, however, the poems move in the direc-
tion of quarrels that are neither fully realized nor transformed
from harangues. John Berryman, for one, saw possibilities within
Garrigue even while he struggled to define her style. "I . . . feel
inclined to be quiet and see what she does or her poems do. She
is not quite in the Climate."[16] The statement might have held for
Garrigue's entire career; she was willfully out of "the Climate"
and preferred, seemingly, to remain so. The collection is polem-
ical in its analysis of postwar sensibilities and in arguments
between the nature of intellect and of sensation, the personal ego
and the fabulous hybrid, the centaur of the imagination.

With the publication in 1953 of her third book,*The Monument
Rose,* Garrigue took a distinctly different turn, returning more
confidently to the image and ushering in some elements of archa-
ism until she sounded remotely like one of the female trou-
badors. The volume elegizes the end of early youth. It is the most
ornate, ritualized, and stylistically dense of her books.

A Water Walk by Villa d'Este (1959) is adamant in making joy
from sorrow and positing artistic authority. The metrics loosen,
without the nearly "sprung" rhythms of *The Monument Rose.*
The book celebrates transfiguration and redeemed time. In a
similar vein, *Country Without Maps* (1964) exhibited frequently
European locales but seems a more mature book in which places
and things become loved ones. Her "country without maps" is a
site in the imagination located through the strength of desire.

In 1967 *New and Selected Poems* appeared, culling fifty poems
from previous volumes and adding twenty-four more. The new
work seems a compilation of styles with the imagistic richness of
The Monument Rose and the conversational openness of *A Water
Walk by Villa d'Este.*

In her final collection, *Studies for an Actress and Other Poems* (1973), Garrigue enacted a partial self-accounting. The book is shadowed by the death of her mother, that of her intimate friend the novelist Josephine Herbst (1897–1969), the memory of her father's death, and Garrigue's awareness of her own mortality. The collection is her handbook on loss. The poems more openly engage autobiographical materials and political concerns. She is critical of commercialism and waste and revitalizes her faith in transformation through the imagination.

As Louise Bernikow reminded us over a decade ago, "What is commonly called literary history is actually a record of choices."[17] Given Garrigue's position as one of the more prominent American women poets at midcentury, knowledge of her work deepens and extends our thinking about poetic tradition. But surely in her own right Garrigue is a significant American poet whose plurality of vision deserves reappraisal. More than ten years ago Stanley Kunitz suggested that "another generation may be better tuned" to "the freshness" of Garrigue's voice.[18] To be "tuned" to this voice requires that we rethink our critical conceptions, for Garrigue continually falls between our notion of types. She asks of us a form of double vision akin to what Rachel Blau du Plessis, in another context, calls "a both/and vision born of shifts, contraries, negations, contradictions." Later critics often appear unfamiliar with Garrigue's striking earlier work, with its use of traditional aspects of prosody as an exemplar of the difficulty of correspondence. And yet to many earlier, more traditional critics, Garrigue's poems seemed close to undirected, nearly formless, her mixture of the sublime and the common discomfitting.

As John Frederick Nims has it, "Speech is a tweedy fabric; verse is a twill."[19] If so, Garrigue's poetry is often composed of a remarkable double thread. She worked deliberately to evade standard critical programs and available poetic genres and resisted the objectification of experience and of others. Through complicating perspectives, she cancelled out her own "possession." Her evasions amount to both a victory and a hazard; we would, perhaps, have heard more of her work if she had not refused to be self-consistent. A plurality of treatment, however, seemed essential: "Anything twice looked at becomes enormously complex" (Berg), a character in her unpublished novel declares. Garrigue's speakers heroically confront their own unsatisfied and sometimes contradictory desires. Among her papers, a note characterizes the volatility of her searches:

Life is a lonely thing in many ways[.] We're born into families and
fight to get away from them, and born into an organized world that is
just a pretense over chaos and born into people that don't satisfy the
heart, and keep it hungry all day and all week and all year, and then
we go out looking and looking and we don't know what it is we'll be
looking for. . . . And the search remains unending.   (Berg)

This poet's focus on an "unending" search echoes her commitment to enact dramas of desire without possession. She imag-
ined a poetic search as a visual quest ("we go out looking and
looking") but often one of unembodied "possibility"—and surely
in her terms such a quest "does not end." In a letter to Ruth
Herschberger she defined herself as working from "the point of
view of one who could never consort with the conventions"
(Berg). Characteristically, her poems complicate chronology, for
the present moment is not only saturated with the past but with
future intimation. She imagines moments when memory and
desire intersect, but finally she is suspicious of revelation. This
suspicion is reflected not only in shiftings of perspective within
poems and her changes in style but in poems in which revelation
eludes the speaker as in "Grief was to Go Out, Away." The poem
makes both its statement of faith and its acceptance of vision's
curtailment before mortality.

> . . . as if it were dying, [we] run to embrace
> Our life lying out there, misadventured, abstruse,
> In the great wedge of light beamed forth
> Like messengers sallying out
> To your "I see! I see!" bearing a scroll
> On which the word is almost decipherable.
>
>   (SFA, 73)

The poet lives in the wavelike rhythm between almost knowing
and surely not knowing; the poem serves as both an article of
faith and a warning against assuming one absolute.

As one of the few women whose poems attained critical attention before the second wave of feminism, Garrigue's position is
especially interesting. Her poems, in their ectastic tensions, are
atypical. She admired Marianne Moore's propensity to illuminate particulars and what Garrigue terms Moore's "delicate,
taxing technique" (MM, 5) and her "zest for the idiosyncratic"
(MM, 41). She was more often than Moore, however, a poet of the
nonrational. Unlike Moore's and Elizabeth Bishop's, her poems

are often openly erotic and announce themselves as a woman's texts. Like Bishop, she chose to write of her foreign travels and she felt herself an exile in sensibility from many of her contemporaries.

Significantly, Garrigue did not turn from certain aspects of the women's tradition that Cheryl Walker defines in The Nightingale's Burden: Women Poets and American Culture Before 1900. Instead she would reproduce, in particular, strands of intensive feeling, what Walker calls "the sensibility poem," a poem "in which a woman defines herself in terms of her immoderate and often agonized sensitivities."[20] Garrigue valorizes sheer feeling, one resource culturally alotted women, and yet she revises the sensibility poem of her predecessors by increasingly placing convention under pressure. She interrogates, for instance, romance, displaying irony toward both the self and the love partner. And she betrays no significant ambivalence toward her own desires for freedom, as Walker notes of an earlier generation of women within their "power fantasies"; avidly and repeatedly she makes transformative and radiantly connective power a focus of poems. She was in turn angered by the treatment of women writers, as her notes, collected in the Berg Collection of the New York Public Library, suggest:

> Known for the difficulty of having hair—women writers. For no propensity toward dance. If men and children make up their destinies, then for the e[f]fort of going against that grain. Targets of rebuke by men. "You are such a child!" laughing. "Come now, no self-pity." Coldly. (Berg)

Her notes on the comments of a man who derided her work point up her sense of trespass: "don't staple my reins enough to earth, am not self contained enough, am too much the fountain wind, unreined and therefore in competition with men" (Berg). Such criticism did not, pointedly, diminish her ambitions. Garrigue developed her own distinctive poetic landscape, writing of actresses, webs, forests, walks, and refusing self-containment. Throughout her career the poet turned to central motifs, developing her art through a sustained vocabulary of recurrent images. By focusing on such motifs in this study, I hope to suggest both the intricacy and integrity of Garrigue's most realized poetry.

Garrigue's central motifs reflect her preoccupations with vision and generosity, women's imaginative power, love relationships, and the authority of desire. The first chapter of this study ex-

plores this poet's insistence on composing "multiple exposures."
Particularly within studies of art, politics, and animals, Jean
Garrigue investigates the never-innocent act of seeing. Enamored
with appearances, she creates "trials" for the scanning eye. Peculiar to her preoccupation with involved seeing is not only her
self-consciousness about sight as an active choice but her search
to widen identification between the "seer" and the seen.

Through her focus on performers, discussed in the second
chapter, Garrigue will not transcend plurality but initiates "multiple centers," the plurality of being suggested by Luce Irigaray:
"(Re-)discovering herself, for a woman, . . . could only signify the
possibility of sacrificing no one of her pleasures to another, of
identifying herself with none of them in particular, *of never
being simply one.*"[21] Through her poems in which women dominate a scene, Garrigue discovered an image of a woman who is
ungovernable; if she is a subject it is to godlike beings or a
collective unconscious, both associated with the imperatives of
art; if she is harried by their imperatives she has also been
singularly successful at evoking their cooperation. Her figures,
superficially resembling conventional muses, do not as in the
male tradition usher in vision capriciously and are themselves
incapable of creativity. If muselike in their effects on others—
releasing awareness of imaginative potential—they act as creators
on their own behalf.

In her poems on love, explored in the third chapter, Garrigue
traces the restless imagination in romance. She criticizes a cate-
gorizing intellect that would render experience inert. Through
her almost obsessive focus upon the word "heart" Garrigue paradoxically suggests both the power of romance to feed the active
poetic imagination and the imagination's capacity to overwhelm
the actual lover through the very force of the imagination.

A final chapter explores Garrigue's water walks. In poems organized around walks beside water or in contemplations of natural processes in metaphors of fluidity, Garrigue finds an analogue
for the desirous imagination. If water for this poet is a kind of
poetic resource that the poem describes and emulates, through
the walk's changing landscape and the variable consciousness of
the walker, speakers discover the range of their own authority as
it is manifested through desire.

Garrigue emerges as a poet of elusive multiplicity, imagining a
plenitude that both enriches and evades. In *Women as Mythmakers* Estella Lauter isolates a condition akin to Garrigue's:

If the central issue of myth for men has been to triumph over the threat of nothingness, then the central issue for the women I treat here is significantly different. Tentatively, I would describe it as a tension between the multiplicity of being (experienced often as an overflow of images, feelings or thoughts) and the man-made structures that are supposed to order being and give it meaning. Instead of a wasteland, we have here a landscape teeming with interwoven forms of life, whose affinity with our own form we need only recognize to enjoy.[22]

Garrigue travels through such "interwoven forms of life," making her route "From the cat to the horse by way of the dragon" (CWM, 5). The opulence of Garrigue's poetry suggests some of the "disruptive power" that Nina Auerbach speculates upon: "For women . . . character remains the promise of a 'fabulous opera,' holding the inspiration of becoming the creature of one's own creation, of stepping out of an imposed frame."[23] Garrigue's poetry, so often a poetry of plenitude, doublings, and multiple perspectives, enacts a performance of self-creation.

1

"THE EXCESSIVE LANGUAGE OF LIGHT"

Jean Garrigue's "Restless Eye"

The eye of Jean Garrigue's poetry is the amazed, "restless eye." In a 1944 introduction to her poems, Garrigue wrote that hers is a "medium which allows gracious license to the fluctuations, recoils and most delicate expeditions. . . . [W]ith perfecting of the medium comes increased sensitivity to the varieties of insight, to the possibilities of play with them, play on them . . ." (*TSP,* 85). The poet's choice of the word *expeditions* is characteristic. She remains aware that sight is never simple or innocent but involves both conscious and unconscious sources; as John Berger reminds us, sight invokes choice.[1] Garrigue's sophisticated eye explores multiple contours, suggesting the limits of visibility; something forever evades sight. Yet whatever finally evades the "restless eye" in Garrigue's poetry is less to be mourned than to be celebrated. Her eye submits to trials as, in her words, "appearance intersects with all the memoranda the poet is urgently stirred to relate to it . . ." (*TSP,* 86).

   In Garrigue's motif, the eye is the self poring over surfaces and in effect "reading" them. An analysis of her preoccupation with questions of sight provides an introduction to some of her most accomplished poetry. Over the more than thirty years of her career, Garrigue's most engaged seeing operates as a form of dare in which the poet as eye identifies with what is seen as "all the flesh becomes an eye." By transforming the self into an eye, she dilates the self and suggests the growth of possibility through identification between the seer and the seen. Rendering both the self and the focus of sight as open to possibility—open to continually renewing margins and thresholds—requires an ability to explore multiple surfaces. To see as Garrigue sees means to distrust static perceptions and to plunge the eye into the glancing effects of light. There is no simplistic or confining "photographic clarity" in the object of sight or the seeing eye/I. Through fluctuating transformations, the poet renders the eye as the "I" of manifold identity.

Among the poems that reveal her fascination with questions of sight, Garrigue's "The Grand Canyon" takes special place. After Garrigue was found in 1971 to have Hodgkin's disease, she traveled from California, where she held a teaching position, to undergo treatment in the East. On her way she made her first trip to the Grand Canyon, a trip that resulted in one of her most fully realized poems. Here the poet as an eye continually sees form amid chaos. Garrigue's canyon is ultimately a volatile test for the eye in which the poet recognizes the limits of the sense of sight before the void: for her "the total effect [is] never total for never can you see it all, not even guess / at mazes of the proliferation" (SFA, 69). The curious pleasure of naming and beginning to "see" and to "guess" "mazes of the proliferation" animates the poem. Before the canyon, the poet's eye takes on the status of a slippery-legged insect, an image that suggests both the vulnerability and the dexterity of the eye:

> . . . the eye like a long-legged insect on a windowpane
> slithers and shudders up and down
> the banded and ribboned, ribbed systems of rock,
> into and out of shadows,
> chromatic world of what glitters like phantoms. . . .
>
> (71)

This volley into seeing occurs in contradisctinction to the canyon's very emptiness, its aspect as void or absence, and its "rocky silence," the "pure condition of the original *echoing* soundlessness" (69; emphasis mine). Against the canyon's echoing and thus doubled silence, Garrigue places the poem's visual "volubility." Her canyon becomes a voluminous artwork, the void a basin for form in the poet's tour de force, opening with a one-line question, a nine-line sentence, a half-line question, and finally a one-hundred-and-ten-line sentence, an extensive drive against both silence and our expectations of closure.

Here the eye hovers over extinction, "this voluminous wrung resonance" (69):

> . . . I came to the edge and looked over:
> violaceous, vermillion

great frontal reefs, buttes,
cliffs of rufous and ocher angles,
promontories, projections, jutments, outjuttings
and gnarled mirlitons, so it seemed
twisting up out of depth beyond depth
gnarled like the juniper tree
rachitic with wind I hung on to
as the raven's wing, glassy in the light of its black,
slid over me. . . .

                                                                        (68)

The eye, like the raven's wing, "darts" into "the light on that
chaos of creases" (69). Laurence Lieberman observes that Garrigue "would be a voyaging essence, contained and uncontaina-
ble, hitching a ride—a cosmic hitchhiker—on forms, animate or
inanimate."[2] Such an act of all-out seeing submits the speaker to
risk and violence. The juniper tree and the poetic self together
become "rachitic," the latter inflamed with both the movements
of the canyon's wind and the task of seeing into a void from
which she calls up images of natural and artificial forms.

The eye, focusing on the effects of light, follows and becomes a
form of light. As the eye travels in "mazes of . . . proliferation (69)
light becomes, like the eye, a thing of "nerves": "the gold of the
light on that chaos of creases nervously darts" (69). Four line-
groupings later Garrigue repeats the action, reiterating "the gold
on the light nervously darting" (70). As Anne Hollander has
written, "The moving eye is the other half of moving light, the
analogue of the seeking heart and searching mind."[3] The canyon
tests the eye as identity, as the "I." A "gash" or giant opening, the
canyon provides the ultimate subversion of closure.

"The Grand Canyon" evolves as a Mobius strip of sorts, its
opening a "return" from the void. Garrigue spans her canyon and
yet must eventually return to the evanescent world of the living.
The speaker now desires to be among others, beyond the solitude
of the nonliving forms of stone. The light by which she then sees
will be "fluorescent," made by humans. Tellingly, her speaker is
lonely, for the sublime has prompted her to yearn for community
and kinship. This yearning often follows Garrigue's expeditions
into far seeing. While tracing the patterns of sight she suggests
that the concentration of seeing will in fact have created the need
for kinship:

I am lonely under the fluorescent light
as a cook waddles in her smoky region visible through an
     open arch

and someone is pounding, pounding
whatever it is that is being pounded
and a waitress cracks with the cowboys lined up at the
    counter
lumberjacked, weathered and bony
intimates, I would guess, of the Canyon,
like the raven that flies, scouting above it,
of the hooked face and the almost flat sleek wings.

(68)

Visually on the page, the speaker's ways of seeing render the Grand Canyon as multiple and fluid, a kind of ziggurat, or as fountainlike, ascending and descending in plays of scale. The eye submits to vertigo, and a single, solitary focus is radically upended before the vastness of the canyon. Throughout her description, the speaker is threatened by the canyon's silence and depth. Yet she catalogues its multitude of shapes in human terms; she becomes the void's "seer" who metamorphoses rough stone into accomplished form.

The contrasts in the poem range from gargantuan forms to the smallest markings as eras are reflected in canyon walls. Natural incorporation is a powerful "terror" to the eye that must see so inclusively:

the blond Coconino sandstone
[is] riddled, it's said, with the trails of sea worms,
on the grey Kaibab limestone
with casts of shark teeth and horn coral imbedded
. . . with footprints of salamanders, insect wings four
    inches in length
and even a dimple left by a raindrop during some era of
    burning

(70)

In the poem's final image a cloud moves over the canyon, a technique of open-ended closure reminiscent of the earlier "Pays Perdu" of Country Without Maps (1964). Garrigue echoes the shape of her own experience, moving from the solidified mass to the disappearance of the "envisioned":

the stillness
pressed in by the gorged rock
deepening in the light of the motes of beams
under those clouds that like water lilies

enclose within them this silence received
that they graze upon and are gone.

(71)

In one of the earliest descriptions of her work, Garrigue writes
that the poet hopes to make in words "signs for an impalpable
imponderable that one seeks to get down before all evaporates."[4]
The canyon has become an "impalpable imponderable," beyond
the power of description. Her final simile of cloud and lilies
suggests that all that is fragile and evanescent refreshes stone.
The eye-self, "the motes of beams," are also "the motes of being."
The atomized self hovers above the canyon's stone. Such "motes"
enact a pointillism; the elastic self becomes, through the poem's
giant final sentence, able to span the canyon, to span its representation of time and its actual distance, and finally to rise like a
cloud above the stone. Silence, now a "silence received," reverses Garrigue's original evocations until the self seeks re-
plenishment among mortal voices and mortal time—away from
spatialized time as it is apparently revealed by the canyon's
geologic traces. The eye that sees becomes, in the eye/I pun, the
self that witnesses its own plurality by viewing and releasing
forms, the self that in its scanning makes even stone dynamic.

Throughout her poetry Garrigue draws attention to the act of
seeing, the particularly threatening and frightening task of viewing in terms of relationship, to see, as in the canyon, "era stacked
upon era," by remaining sensitive to the ways in which the
present moment relates to the past. In seeing time spatialized she
enacts "a tension pitched between the eye and time." She discloses the eye's movement upon the conventionally static stone
as quick movement, for nothing truly and actively seen, Garrigue
would have us know, is static. Within this act, the eye becomes
what it sees; the eye turns into an extension of the canyon,
capable of making and casting up form after form. Light perme-
ates the self; eye as identity becomes as encompassing as light.
The eye, then, is Garrigue's set-upon sense. The eye as well as
the "I" must seize upon a strategy so that the eye will not "frame"
the image but scan it to follow patterns in change. The "scoundrel eye," "the murderer eye," "the restless eye," the eye "shat-
tered" by "time's emblems" must not be the imperialist that owns
and objectifies all it sees. It must prompt insight and intimation.
"The Grand Canyon" dares death, for the eye seems to travel with
the unhampered agility we might believe to be appropriate to a

disembodied spirit. Yet Garrigue's speaker returns to the warmth and camaraderie of a restaurant after she has faced the canyon, out of respect and need for the living, the humble, and the close-at-hand. She composes exercises in compassion and kinship; in seeing with Garrigue, we may see more passionately—and in more dimensions than we might otherwise—for seeing "is to be enlarged . . . , to gain light from a mind."

In a selection from an unpublished novel, Garrigue makes one of her primary characters "the only woman *optist* in America." The eyeballs that the woman makes for "gentlemen" prove curiously vulnerable, for they are "button-shaped things, looking more like cold oysters than anything else, who roll slightly together when trucks rumble by, shaking as they usually do, the frail component parts of this house."[5] Garrigue interrogates the "frail component parts" of vision; there is more to be "known" than the eye allows—as her Romantic forebears would insist—and yet it is through the function of the eye that we are able to gain strikingly broad "varieties of insight." Her speakers emerge as involved witnesses to and participants within scenes, self-critically aware in sophisticated acts of shape-making.

Her speakers are often compelled by reflecting, light-filled structures that dazzle the eye. Dazzling light not only becomes an agent of refreshment but also destroys the imperial vision of the unified self in baffling multiplicity. Light pours into the poems explicitly as movement, as an agent that leads toward growth (as light, indeed, must in nature). The eye turns into a "scoundrel" when it settles upon a derivative vision, where the sensual has become heavy and deadening. There must be a "further seeing" or a further seeking inspired in part by "The long coil of the past— . . . bearing upon the immediacy of the moment."[6] The speaker attempts a form of visual concentration, for she knows that seeing is never simple.

Hyatt H. Waggoner explains a similar metaphorics that invests perception:

Common sense and ordinary language encourage us to distinguish between "seeing" and "seeing *as*," but if the retinal image is "inherently ambiguous," as [vision research John P.] Frisby and the others tell us, where do we draw the line between the matter-of-fact and the metaphoric? If seeing even at the most literal level involves interpreting signals and perceiving relationships, then the metaphoric language of poetry need not be merely "emotive" or decorative, as the positivists would have it, lacking the "truth-value" of statements of fact, but noetic, meaningful.[7]

In Garrigue perception requires all the resources the poet can bring to bear upon the act. All the poet's talents and massive "fortifications" of craft must from within the network of the poem seem delicately precise, and the poet must reveal the act of seeing as fraught with the most selective of near double exposures.

Garrigue's meditation on Lucas Cranach the Elder's *Nymph of Spring* within her 1970 collection of prose poems reveals an aesthetics of seeing that relies on such juxtaposition: "the little blonde with crooked legs lying so much in the foreground she is about to fall out of it . . . into whose arms? Who wants this wizened witch face . . . ?" Yet in the distance, nearly appearing afloat, is the "platonic city," as it is "opposed to her density, specificity, her embodied bodily readiness" (*C&PP*, 47). The idyllic needs its flesh, its living core; the ideal lends an airiness to portraiture that might appear turgid, while the fully fleshed in its peculiar livingness supports this sort of vault work. As seeing is not a neutral activity, neither is writing. These are capricious activities, and the discovery initiates renewed extensions of selfhood, suggesting the possibility of freedom rather than mere mastery. The active eye sees both the blonde and the city; both fleshiness and the dream of perfection, the concretely real and the ideal. Seeing enacts an expedition; there are few "givens." The "little blonde" is going to evade framing; she will not be objectified. She is "about to fall" out of the frame.

Garrigue's poetry, in turn, is written to evade the frame of passive response. Like the actress she wrote of in her posthumously published collection, Garrigue must always be "acting the whole part out" through multiple figures and multiple perspectives. Her voice "arises from a deep local dislocation" (*N&SP*, 156) in a poetry that is wittily, sometimes earnestly, enamoured of surfaces.

Just as she envisions a multiple self rather than a single unitary self, Garrigue sees within individual figures in art a plenitude. Her titles suggest generosity: "A Figure for J. V. Meer," "Cortège for Colette," "An Improvisation upon the Theme of the Lady and the Unicorn." The seeing eye, the sense that apprehends the painting and the printed word, makes community through inquiry and enthusiasm, its modes of seeing anything but impersonal. When artwork is her generative subject, Garrigue improvises freely, using multiple images to suggest plurally resonant selves. A tapestry poem, "An Improvisation upon the Theme of the Lady and the Unicorn," presents many more figures than are actually woven into the original, already richly figured, tapestries in Paris. Within such poems, a blazing light suggests that the eye gains "illumination" through accretion. The eye encounters more and more light, but illumination does not render the object or the "seer" as unitary. Instead, light permits poet and reader sympathetically to expand: light allows the eye to extend itself upon multiple surfaces.

Titled in the singular, "A Figure for J. V. Meer" actually presents multiple exposures of figures engaged in "conversations" with other presences and finally transformed into the soul "in its chamber." The female figure is illuminated as light pours upon light, and each figure, despite the singularity of the title, proliferates into multiple possibilities of women:

> She who weighs pearls, who plays lutes
> By the crimson rug on a table,
> By the chair with lions reared on its back
> Standing, posed, facing the full fall of light
> There over her left shoulder,
> Or interrupted at music, or clasping a book
> In a yellow jacket bordered by ermine,
> Or in a blue robe, leaves far voluted the color of blue
> In her hair,
> In her hand the slender gold trumpet,
> By a sloping dish, a peach divided in half, . . .
>
> (WW, 26)

The relationship of the "many-jointed" is at the center of this tribute to van der Meer and to his light-filled phenomenal world. Things in their radiance are brought forward in an opening catalogue, each element—pearls, jacket, robe, trumpet, peach, spinet, studs—brimming with light. Garrigue's sense of revelation as untranslatable light dominates the multiple scene, "As if deep back in the interior / Enclosed by the coffered rim / Gildings from the illuminations, / Figures in gold-leaf flame, / Returned through translucence again" (WW, 27). Entering a nearly blinding field, the self, as in Garrigue's free translation of van der Meer, becomes light.

Garrigue's art "reflections" evoke "the excessive language of light." To be "excessive" is to evade, even within the artwork, framed as it is, the further "frame" of simple categorization or passive response. Garrigue's are not so much moments of photographic clarity as of blinding energy: the eye is tested in its capacity to absorb and structure meaning. Light may obscure

rudimentary form but reveal transmuting, nearly fibrous otherworldly images. "The excessive language of light" calls up images of the multitudinous self and multitudinous possibility. To
"exceed" boundaries, the poet identifies selfhood with light,
which cannot be "held" conventionally but radiates to fill space.

Throughout her poetry, Garrigue expresses respect for and
identification with caged or domestic animals, resisting sentimentalization. By seeing as an animal, as the absolutely mar-
ginalized, she further tests the eye, questioning the ways in
which "vision" may be reduced culturally and privately. Dis-
allowed full access to light and free movement, these animals are
seen in detail as disempowered, particularly in sight. Sight may
arise "from a deep local dislocation" among animals that have
been domesticated, caged, or otherwise made unnatural. Garrigue's treatment of animals frequently requires another sort of
"seeing through" in which these animals become "eyes."

Garrigue reports upon animals' captivity and marginalization,
suggesting a similar "reduction" of women and men. As Berger
has it, the "reduction of the animal, . . . is part of the same
process as that by which men have been reduced to isolated
productive and consuming units."[8] Garrigue records that marginalization and objectification; her animals are most often
within cages, their sight—the sense by which they are chiefly
and repeatedly identified—rendered feeble.

Such animals exist as "objects" to be "looked at" within a
reductive power dichotomy. Since they are simply "sights" to be
seen, their own power for seeing is distorted or weakened. The
Himalayan grackle with a "lacklong eye" diminishes daily
within his cage. The ring-necked pheasant sees with a "snake
eye." A portrait of "faithful sick-eyed dogs . . . / Visibly thin, and
shivering off more weight" concludes a reel of cinematic images.
The speaker in the fablelike "The Maimed Grasshopper Speaks
Up" complains of his eyes' broken armor: "The biggest eyes, with
armor on, / That gave me fore and backward sight / Into the
ditches of rash thought / Serve me not" (MR, 25). The poem
includes five quatrains, the sixth stanza a trimeter as if it too were
broken armor. The grasshopper interrogates his fate, ending with
a bitter prayer: "World without end, commend me to your might /
That I my simple eyes may set / On it, or death, or hate, and get
some light." Garrigue's grasshopper pursues sight at any cost,
even if his simple eyes would reveal only the partial truths of
"death" or "hate." Similarly, in "A Note to La Fontaine" (CWM,

31) Garrigue rewrites the tale of the ants and the grasshopper to support the grasshoppers' prodigality. Her grasshoppers will not live in deferred time; they will continue "spitting into the bleak eye" of limited sight.

"Modern zoos are an epitaph to a relationship which was as old as man,"[9] Berger writes. And to pass among cages, as Berger points out, is similar to making one's way through an art gallery. "In principle, each cage is a frame."[10] In two postwar poems Garrigue writes of zoo animals as if they were "objects" of sight, yet she radically upends her own earlier metaphors by insisting on a complex sense of displacement.

"Iowa City Zoo" (E&C, 83) contemplates the dominant squalor and a peculiar humanlike domesticity among zoo animals. Identification is assumed as Garrigue marks a scene of a rabbit and his "wife," among "leaky houses." At the poem's climactic moment a deer's blindness signals human blindness: "But wall-eyed deer, the lilacs fed you well. / Since you are blind, your eyes are all of us. / When will we trip and fall upon their look, / That bugled eye, that marble-sick uniqueness?" The spectators become "blind"; reduction of the animal amounts to reduction of the human. Yet for the animal Garrigue retrieves dignity even in confinement. The deer, like Garrigue's conception of the poet, feeds on lilacs; he discovers sustenance beyond his miserly confines. The resulting tone accommodates recognition, a certain shame, and, conversely, pride: "marble-sick uniqueness" is better than none at all.

A more achieved poem, "False Country of the Zoo" (E&C, 19–21) links the human and the animal again through the freshness of linguistic surprise and, most revealingly, through complex play on sight. Intricate eye imagery and direct references to the eye reflect Garrigue's ability to fuse and then decategorize response. The animals are, first of all, viewed in metaphorical relationship; the emu's "small head shakes like an old woman's eye"; the secretary bird runs "like a long-legged boy in short pants" and then "on his toes" metamorphoses into "part gasping girl" (19). The kangaroo "walks like a cripple" (20). The cassowary, ostrich, and emu "survive like kings, poor antiquated strays" (20). As Babette Deutsch notes, these "pictures . . . might have been drawn with Marianne Moore's delicate pencil."[11] If the zoo is an arena for a visitor who must acknowledge anthropomorphic kinship, it is also a scene for the senses, particularly sight. In the first image of an individual animal, Garrigue has played upon a cliché: "With the gazelle we long to look eye to eye" (19). That this looking is not accomplished is part of the pathos of the poem. Garrigue's master stroke emerges in her doublings. The "eye" admits pity for the animals' commodified status and recognition of a similar status for women and men. The moment to honor emotion resists sentimentalization as Garrigue doubles the copula:

> The peacock, plumes up, though he walks as if weighted
> —All that unconscionable tapestry—
> Till a wind blows the source of his pride
> And it becomes his embarrassment,
> The eye, plunged in sensation, closes.
> Thought seizes the image. This shrieking
> Jungle of spot, stripe, orange,
> Blurs. The oil from the deer's eye
> That streaks like a tear his cheek
> Seems like a tear, is, is,
> As our love and our pity are, are.
>
>   (21)

The peacock, beauty's symbolic bird, lifts a "tapestry" of eyes, a particularly effective eye/I pun given the peacock's pride. The "eye" of the peacock's tail, as Deutsch points out, is as well the human eye. The tear is "oil from the deer's eye" and yet a tear. Pity dilates the self. Peacock eye, deer eye, human eye, the eye as arbiter would shut against the truth of the moment but opens immediately, widening identification. The very "slipperiness" of seeing and the rejection of the utility of a single-placed reference animate the poem. Both zoo poems close with images of deer, suggesting not only the rare and the costly but also the deer as an animal whose outstanding quality of fleetness is particularly antithetical to confinement. Without the ability to fulfill innate capacities, the animal is "blind." A similar reduction affects women and men; deer and human interpenetrate in a moment that amounts to double vision, a realization of the confinement of both the one who witnesses this degradation and the living animal as the confined object of sight.

   " 'I believe in what I do not see," Garrigue quotes the novelist and activist Josephine Herbst in "In Memory" (SFA, 21). Through late poems focusing on political struggle Garrigue attempts to most fully witness the present moment and to celebrate political resistance. Bringing to sight nuanced political concerns becomes the task she sets for herself: "You pin your nerve to your luck." "It is this you were meant for / Opening the door to the sweating shadow / Quickly, quietly, in the structured maze" (SFA, 60). Entering the "maze" of committed seeing that enables action is foremost among her late poems that dramatize political consciousness.

What can be seen in public displays of political resistance? How may political struggle free the eye for visual inquiry and acts of transformation? By employing the sort of scanning and multiple exposures prominent in poems in which she "becomes an eye," Garrigue witnesses contemporary turmoil and resists collapsing into simplified theory. Her final poems confront the long war in Indochina, despoilation of the environment, and throughout, the poverty of images by which we live in the contemporary world. The poems move toward envisioning a present that may create momentum to make a more resonant future possible. Like Herbst, Garrigue could say, "I believe in what I do not see." In these late poems she also believes in what she does see—and dramatizes the discipline of visual inquiry.

In poems assuming multitudinous selves and multiple ways of being, Garrigue politicized the personal. Her overtly political "vision" evolves through her effort to unite public struggle, particularly that against the Vietnam War and ecological disaster, with "the dream of fair men and women" (SFA, 59). Garrigue's poems engage politics with more dream-inspired states, areas of being that are conventionally "recessed." Early poems rely on her perception of injustice and cultural depletion. "Our armless men are all our statues now," Garrigue wrote in "V-J Day" (E&C, 27), one of her earliest poems from the 1940s that is explicitly political and tellingly upholds monument art as a register of public well-being. Garrigue looks warily at Victory over Japan Day celebrations, questioning national gaiety. She is aware of despoilation of nature, the "cruisers smoking offshore" ("Enemy of the Body," E&C, 62) and the consequences of crowding in cities. She writes of an anti-Semitic beating and the community's response, "fragmented" by its aftershock. In "Poem" she evokes an ideal that admits change as requisite to transcendence even in a political and urban climate that stultifies: "Immutable vision of the beautiful / That changes once and once again with light!" (E&C, 65).

Among later poems, Garrigue's political meditations turn to activity but not simple polemic. As early as 1939 Garrigue had expressed herself against the programmatic. She supported Louise Bogan in the poet's early days as poetry editor of the New

Yorker for opposing "soapbox poetry and conversion of Marxism to metaphor, the lament for a tired reliefer, and all that."[12] Significantly, in "Police of the Dead Day" (*N&SP*, 156) she takes on the persona of cat-activist, an animal bristling with back alley life, "In the dirt and the dark, turning corners. . . ." She stands to be stripped of an enveloping knowledge for, as she writes in "Swiss Altitude," the soul must either discover or invest "a wildness whose glance no civilization may endure" (*WW*, 20).

In her final book Garrigue newly calibrates her political growth, culminating with poems in which she "becomes an eye" to encompass public political movements and reconcile aesthetics with political necessity. Within this final series she recounts her own journey from despair to a questioning form of activity, moving from resignation to vision. Through her struggle to deal with ecological disaster and the ongoing Vietnam War she unites an intensive privacy with public images. She enacts ways of seeing in the protest march, the meeting, and other forms of organized resistance. The opening poem of the fourth section of *Studies for an Actress* asks the question, "May only the ugly drive out the ugly?" (*SFA*, 53). Her aesthetic question signals her revulsion from any vision that would not incorporate resonant forms. The early, digressive, nearly self-defeating lines descend into parenthetic tenderness:

> (Take my hand, darling,
> Be not what I prey on
> That preys on me, or . . . .)
>
> (54)

The action is identical to that between dying mother and daughter in the same volume's "Dry Summer—1965": hand-holding against the dark. This poem's very inconclusiveness reveals her hesitancy to project programmatic solutions and yet prepares us for poems that move away from lamentation into complex realization, away from evasion to contemplate risk.

With the second poem in her series, "Lead in the Water" (*SFA*, 55), Garrigue descries ecological decline and technological excess for "escape artists" who are "still cuddling picture postcards of the ideal." The ideal is reduced to simple photographic duplication, without the rigor of the enlarging visual energies that Garrigue sought. The following poem, one of the most successful of the series, " 'For Such a Bird He Had No Convenient Cage' " moves toward a more complex response. She examines the convictions of a woman whose "dreameries had been raided":

> It was the pain of others beginning to show through,
> It was angst about their almost inhuman bravery,
> It was hearing the wound gnaw in them,
> Phagocytes at the stormed body.
>
> (SFA, 56)

Public life had failed to register Garrigue's reflection: "It was the pain of others beginning to show through." The woman whose "dreameries had been raided" knows her depletion through the training she has given her eye. She is prepared to see "hostilities [that] had everywhere to hide." She has been taken to far thresholds of selfhood and yet her own private intensities have been subjected to unsympathetic eyes: "To their limits they [her dreameries] had been exposed."

"Free-Floating Report" (SFA, 57–59), while an account of action rather than despair, is Garrigue's explicit return to the question of how to envision a future. Is the future to be construed as the image of a man "going around the corner, his pants blown out by the wind, / That pottering, grey-faced bakery dog"? (58) Is this to replace "the dream of fair men and women" (59)?

What in public life has failed her? Garrigue descries the contemporary emphasis on speed, efficiency, and consumption as well as the denial of images of beauty and achievement that may foster the human dream of "making and re-making" (65). The contemporary public "eye" reduces the living to a limited frame, making even the dog a kind of worker: "That pottering, grey-faced bakery dog." The seeing eye must be conscious that it is the supplementary eye; we bring to what we see our desires and vague intimations of future possibility. Garrigue maintains her belief that the poet must visualize both justice and beauty; the poet as the "restless eye" becomes a self-questioning seeker.

The poem that follows, "The War Has Just Begun (Soliloquy)" (SFA, 60–62), visualizes a nightmarish future, engagement in resistance work, and in guerilla underground tactics. The labyrinthine lines of political assignations reveal new sight; significantly, the "many-eyed labyrinth" (61) of the poem opens onto a window. Political action may irradiate the incoherence of a life. The self is remarkably like a light-filled canvas:

> If we live by fiction, if we keep up to the mark
> For the sight of the quai
> Reflecting that something we cannot say
> Have we not known it before?
> We have not. It is what we would know.
> And if, in the many-eyed labyrinth

> You come to the moment you can no longer avoid,
> Then, without blunder, to meet
> What you have traced over and over in sleep,
> The map of the rivers, the vines, the walls,
> The walls with the windows, to have the design
> Of the thing you have lost suddenly clear,
> Pressing against you,
> Then breaking out
> Into the whole sight
> And your half-finished life finished in it.
>
>   (61–62)

Yet this is not art as a window onto the world. Rather, Garrigue's window admits a "design" "pressing"; the image is similar to the elaborate scrollwork she finds in the medieval window in *Chartres and Prose Poems* and that, elsewhere, the poet acknowledges as that of the eye. The poem explodes the "frame"; the window, only conventionally perceived as opening onto the "real," admits renewed vision, allowing the speaker to reencounter the formerly lost. This is Garrigue's recurrent conception of the artistically attained vision—now reworked and sought through political acts, a "whole-sightedness" that includes the public within the private life. "To be in the windows," to be an eye within an "eye," the "half-finished life finished in it," risks the incorporative force of the art she seeks. The labyrinth or maze is transformed into the eyelike window; the mazelike structures of Garrigue's elaborate poems create "trials" of vision.

In the section's culmination, "Resistance Meeting: Boston Common," (*SFA*, 63–65) Garrigue most directly weds the cultivation of political insight with an artist's multiple, plenitudinous vision. She longs for an eye that can appraise the thresholds of action:

> For those lounging and lolling here,
> what painter will arrest them in their gear,
> at their height of time?
> Not hardened yet or tarnished, standing yet
> upon the grounds of choice,
> still at the moment of decision
> or at the moment before decision.
>
>   (SFA, 64)

Just as the poem experiments with repeated meanings of "order," "reason," and "power," Garrigue multiplies the meanings of "arrest." The painter "arrests" demonstrators with a vision that does not "harden" them. Her artist would reveal them at a moment when they are at a threshold, before immanence. It is this liminal state that has preoccupied the poet.

In this, Garrigue's poem of opening to a collective vision, the self is not obscured by the collective but is about to experience yet another transformation. Sight becomes all-important. "The smog of confusion has lifted. / Now may light shimmer from the tree." The speakers offer pure, spare speech, "the clarity being the astonishment" (63). Public speech is not part of a deadened "entablature" but a light field, "All this on a bud-gemmed day whose luster / the words of the speakers do not wither" (65).

She explores the sense of sight, incorporating contemporary political resistance into aesthetic vision:

> April in the Public Garden.
> The boys who will be drafted are here,
> some bearded like disciples,
> others with the large dark eyes of *The Volunteers of 1792*
> as painted by Thomas Couture,
> horsemen-like as a painter might see them,
> stilling, instilling their fire
> of so much being to be praised by the future.
>
> (63)

Explicitly, the painter's strategy of praise is enviable. The painter projects a heroic image that may nourish both eye and mind. Light effects in their organic settings also reflect self-growth and the freely ranging senses.

In characteristic complexity, Garrigue denies her speaker facile heroism or self-aggrandizement. She understands political impetus not only by seeing draft resisters as they might be treated in an artwork but in images that link death to a new life-giving art in yet another reversal: "blood enamel[s] the pages of the book of some life." Should they not resist, the destruction that the young men would carry out becomes "the jellied fire / and the chemicals depositing arsenic in the soil" (SFA, 65). She links her ecological concerns with political and aesthetic issues. Her cumulative questions mount toward a perception that encompasses past and future, no longer raiding inmost needs; a new "use" of "order" must be encountered that does not make "instruments" of women and men.

The surprisingly quiet, unambivalent, "On Going by Train to White River Junction, Vt." (SFA, 66–67) directly following Gar-

rigue's final section of political poems, suggests another mode of
being: gracious nonappropriation. The poem moves through its
catalogue of nonappropriative movement, after asserting of the
train: "It interferes very little / As it lays down its way," The
poem's movement is similar to the eye's movement. The metaphor suggests an aesthetic vision that discloses without violence:

> Nor removes ledges of sunlight
> On cliffed parallels of rock
> Nor savages nuances of meadow
> Nor rips away mosses in a hollow
> Nor requires that sawn woods stand like so many
>   scorched matchsticks
> Nor musters out ranks of cornstalks
> Nor engorges great swatches of dingle
> Of ostrich fern in the blue-heroned swamp.

> (66)

Following the sequence of political poems, then, this poem suggests a landscape set in the center with an eye:

> You travel with it [the train] and the stones by the river—
> By the tussocked meadows
> With ponds set glittering like an eye
> In the fine lashwork of twigs and boughs in a tangle. . . .

> (66–67)

The water as eye and the eye as water follow a

> . . . course neither mathematically severe
> Nor of the convenience of martial order.
> The scrolls, the cartouche of mists, wisps,
> Breathings in crooks and bends
> Fume out from a hill undismayed by the disarrays of
>   so much unfolding,
> Discontinuous flowing. . . .

> (67)

The actions of the pond-as-eye and the landscape-as-eye suggest
the movements that Garrigue insists upon within political life.
After the suggested violence of the political poems, she brings us
to the natural world and explicitly, through the nonhierarchical
arrangement of the poem's catalogue, takes on a strategy of only
momentary incorporation, for the scene unrolls into light transformations:

> By the green baize of molehills, of ridges,
> In pastures the serene flanks of white horses,
> Under light that dazes and deifies
> Cows winding in among eskers.
>
> (67)

Garrigue's final focus is on the ordinary: farm animals in this light display. Yet the animals are deified; an animal, in fact, that we consider for "use"—the cow as a producer of milk and butter—supplants the traditionally heroic horse. Garrigue returns unobtrusively to a study of light that dilates sensibility.

The poetic self as a fabulous weaver, as the "flesh [that] becomes an eye" identifies with the multiplicity of what is seen. Like her waterspiders, Garrigue's speakers move quickly upon reflecting surfaces and mazes of color, working upon their paths with what Howard Nemerov calls this poet's "curious elaboration of detail."[13] Her personae repeatedly set out on a journey through canyons and canvasses of light, dazzling and testing the scanning eye. To write, as Garrigue has it, is to dare, to attempt expeditions of risk toward "insight." To be large-minded she chooses to be large-eyed. It is a choice that particularly affects, as I hope to show in the next chapter, her conception of women artists.

2
EACH AN "ODD SHE"
Strange Performers

While working on her fourth book as she spent the summer of 1954 traveling in Europe, Garrigue described her poetics in a biographical sketch: "Interior and exterior married in a diagram, a paradigm, by metaphor and rhythm to equate perception with experience. And experience? One takes a complex of experience, trying to deal with as many of its contingents and tangents as the poem will bear. The real is incorrigible, untamable."[1] The statement reflects the conceptual pressure under which Garrigue places the lyric. Such complex ambitions are nowhere more clear than in her poems in which women perform as artists. She presents women as intractable performers seeking to summon and display their own creativity. The implosive quality—the very concentration of such work—suggests this poet's sense of her poetry as an "organized secret," its substance both consciously designed and curiously inviolable. In this context, the elaborate stylization of her female figures serves as a way to disrupt limited perspectives of women's power.

From "The Stranger," one of her earliest and most frequently anthologized poems, to the title poem of her posthumous collection, Garrigue experiments with images of a hybrid self. Just as the lyric speaker for this poet evades self-consistency, so too do her female performers, foregoing singular identity and the claustrophobia of one role. In her personal life Garrigue saw women as powerful artists—including her sister, already an accomplished pianist when Garrigue was born, and through her contemporaries Ruth Herschberger and May Swenson. Her admiration for Marianne Moore, about whom she wrote a critical monograph, and her intimate relationship of about twenty years with the novelist Josephine Herbst further reinforced her preoccupation with the power of women artists. In a culture that denied women's value she countered by presenting artists exercising remarkable authority over others and themselves attaining access to godlike beings. Repeatedly, her poems are dramatizations of women's stature as "alien" and powerful; a woman is a cultural "odd she" whose very struggles reveal her heroism.

An examination of one of Garrigue's earliest poems, "The Stranger," reveals her fascination with a combination of muse and artist—a woman as a stranger who awakens desire as a necessary condition for creation:

> Now upon this piteous year
> I sit in Denmark beside the quai
> And nothing that the fishers say
> Or the children carrying boats
> Can recall me from that place
> Where sense and wish departed me
> Whose very shores take on
> The whiteness of anon.
> For I beheld a stranger there
> Who moved ahead of me
> So tensile and so dancer made
> That like a thief I followed her
> Though my heart was so alive
> I thought it equal to that beauty.
> But when at last a turning came
> Like the branching of a river
> And I saw if she walked on
> She would be gone forever,
> Fear, then, so wounded me
> As fell upon my ear
> The voice a blind man dreams
> And broke on me the smile
> I dreamed as deaf men hear,
> I stood there like a spy,
> My tongue and eyelids taken
> In such necessity.
> Now upon this piteous year
> The rains of Autumn fall.
> Where may she be?
> I suffered her to disappear
> Who hunger in the prison of my fear.
> That lean and brown, that stride,
> That cold and melting pride,
> For whom the river like a clear
> Melodic line and the distant carrousel
> Where lovers on their beasts of play
> Rose and fell,

That wayfare where the swan adorned
With every wave and eddy
The honor of his sexual beauty,
Create her out of sorrow
That, never perishing,
Is a stately thing.

(N&SP, 5–6)

In a situation often dramatized in Garrigue's poems, the speaker does not fully encounter the muselike other but suffers her own regret. The poem moves through interlocking rhyme and assonance as phrases connect easily despite far-reaching associations. Rhymes move closer at the poem's end, a strategy Garrigue frequently employs in a gathering toward closure within shorter lyrics. The frequency of near-rhymes and partial rhymes suggests missed meetings, an elusive echo that just fails correspondence, an effect reinforcing the poem's drama.

"The Stranger" performs on several levels. The stranger is one self-definition of the woman artist; through the image of the stranger Garrigue acknowledges her own cultural "strangeness" as a woman and a poet. "The Stranger," in turn, presents an encounter with a speaker's twin being who makes "the heart the equal beauty." Such a stranger resembles Garrigue's later performers, for she is "dancer-made" and a powerful and fluid other. She is a shadow self before whom a single figure or in later poems an audience may briefly assume emotional equality. Yet such unity is momentary, for her otherness asserts itself. The stranger is, furthermore, a vision; as a figure for poetic inspiration she may not steadily remain before the poet, nor is she conjured at will. Finally, the poem enacts the artist's anxiety in the face of the muse of male tradition, a stranger indeed. As Mary K. DeShazer informs us of the traditional muse: "This enigmatic female figure, whether wise sibyl or chosen lover, exists for the male poet as a series of opposites: he is subject, she is object; he is lover, she is beloved; he is begetter, she is begotten upon."[2] The woman poet's dilemma, as DeShazer reminds us, is particularly complex, for "this tradition of the objectified muse has made it hard for her to transcend her Otherness and thus attain the subjectivity crucial to a strong poetic stance."[3] Garrigue's speaker dramatizes, however, only momentary paralysis. If the speaker is unable to act, from the loss of the stranger she would nevertheless "create her out of sorrow." It is the muse's very disappearance that presents the speaker with opportunity. Paradoxically, her disappearance makes possible the speaker's attempt to create a monument to the muse and, in subterranean form, an analogue for a future self. The speaker has found her alternative to silence. She will not herself become the traditional muse; instead, she will create the poem.

Inspiration in Garrigue's poems may appear as a dream-goddess who invests a sleeping woman with her power, as in "In Praise of that Epic, Dream," or she may emerge as a bride or "empress of hearts" who creates moments of inspired being within her audience. She may be figured as the moon in "Enemy of Those Who Are Enemies of Sleep" (E&C, 79–80) in which the moon is an "empowering glass." In her evocation, Garrigue focuses upon imagery suggestive of those figures of the opera and marriage—the ritualistic opulence and union of opposites that she evokes in her poems about performers:

> Dwarfs, indigo, within whose opera,
> O bridal jest, you circummortal us,
> Nuptial of vacancy who wizards us.
>
> (E&C, 80)

The moon as muse, like the poet, allows us to see the invisibles: "O! how the unknown is big! / O! how the moon gives it skin!" (N&SP, 137). Garrigue finds in the ephemeral moonlight her metaphor for one aspect of the poet's task; the poet puts "skin" on the ineffable.

Power deployed and displayed animates these poems about female authority. As the very stylization of these figures suggests, Garrigue's attraction to female "performers"—whether operatic moons, actual actresses, or brides—rests in her knowledge of the female performer's cultural strangeness and multiplicity of being. Among her undated papers a typed note reflects upon the power of performers: "I thought of all that actors can't do in the attempt to shadow forth imitations of what it is that we are and feel. I thought, too, that in their emblematic roles they 'exonerated' our passions for us, and fulfilled them too. They enacted for us what most of us dared not feel" (Berg). Performers' emotional responsiveness and ability to "enact" diverse spiritual and psychological states intriqued her. She would, consequently, foreground women's power, resilient enough to act out "what most of us dared not feel." The actress, culturally perceived as eccentric, outside the circle of the known and circumscribed, represents both the forbidden and the powerful. We have only to recall the

practice as late as the eighteenth century of refusing burial in
consecrated ground to actresses; their facility in adopting roles
was believed to be made possible by their renunciation of a
singular soul. Even today the actress remains a symbol of fascination, a figure we loosely associate with uncanny power. Garrigue's performers similarly may represent compressed feeling in
poems redolent of the baroque. Babette Deutsch reminds us of
the Portugese root meaning of baroque: "an irregularly shaped
pearl, so that connotations of the bizarre and the opulent seem
appropriate."[4] Irregularly shaped pearls, these poems exhibit
and celebrate female performers' very oddity.

Among the earliest of her poems focusing on ritualized performance, " 'Marriage is a Mystery of Joy' " (E&C, 54–55, and
erratum) presents a bride-poet-performer as informing vision:
"vision seen // From which we wander till we die, never / Ab-
solved in search nor granted solace twice" (55). The bride invokes heightened states of being in others. But unlike the
stranger, she adopts multiple roles. She both acts out a vision and
embodies vision, serving as a reprimand to those who would
refuse their own transformative power. This bride/actress con-
trols illusion before an audience in obeisance to her; like the
actress this poet will invent over two decades later, the bride
intensifies and focuses the emotions of her audience: "Now: we
exist to be her glassy sea, / Not only imagery, but medium / Which
she might drown is as we're drowned, quite lost, / But happy to
be lost, for we are found" (55). She offers her audience the
momentary glimpse of a larger knowledge—an "oddness" that
both poet and audience may seek. The poem then performs as a
kind of conjuring act. Like the stranger, the central figure serves
as the aspiration that the lyric poet seeks in a unity between
opposites, the symbolic marriage prefiguring the dilemma faced
by Garrigue's final actress figure in "Studies for an Actress."

Garrigue presents an actress who enacts her audience's desire
in "The Opera of the Heart: Overture," (MR, 26–28) and yet now
her performer is clearly herself a suffering figure. Conflict is more
readily apparent within her conception of the artist-muse. The
woman is not only "queen" but now she is "beast" and "swan"
"daring in flood those great steps of the heart" (MR, 27). While
the actress inspires visions she may herself be isolated. She
contends with her "dark rooms of the soul":

> You fling against us, break, we see
> All that we shrink from cast on you

> And all its stain blood-sick, and see you go
> From dancing, say, to dark rooms of the soul. . . .
>
> (26)

Playing upon feeling as substance, Garrigue renders emotions as "those maps" which the actress "rule[s]." Shock is a "scar." Passion "overtowers . . . like a far concourse." The heart has "great steps," the music of emotion an "odor." Inhabiting a stage that appears to be part Busby Berkeley inspiration, part enormous exteriorized heart, the actress performs as both a scapegoat and royalty. She is distanced from her audience through her very elaborateness of staging, and she is subject to the will of godlike powers.

Otherworldly figures—chimeras, Venuses, shadows: these will emerge as ever greater presences. Increasingly, her speakers experience moments of unity with spiritual forces and yet suffer their sudden withdrawal. "Your subtle blood so brooding and so taught / By powers borne from out the abyss to us" (28). The later powers are godlike beings: "There stir in the dressing rooms those shades / That search your exile with their lolling hands" (27). The poet acts against ever greater impediments, inner and outer, spiritual, psychological, and cultural. Creativity is portrayed as involving monumental spiritual presences who remain stern and demanding before the actress.

Performers appear sporadically in later poems as if to prepare for Garrigue's most developed work within the actress motif in her final volume *Studies for an Actress*. Performers as out of bounds, beyond the culturally circumscribed, occupy Garrigue's tribute to Isadora Duncan, "On the Legends of a Dancer" (*CWM*, 19) and "For the Circuit of the Orpheum and the Isis" (*CWM*, 23–24) in which "one low voice . . . cries it lives by love." In turn, Josephine Herbst is presented as an actresslike figure living among interconnections in "In Memory"; possessing many selves, she is both a political and a poetic woman, "full of nature" and "indwelling" (*SFA*, 21). She exhibits the qualities of Garrigue's bride-actress-poet: a multiplicity of being and an ability to escape constraints of identity:

> Inside was a you that lived in connections
> Belonging to a thousand persons.
> Putting on them, was that how you learned
> What you really wore,
> Which was joyful wounds, as a poet said?
>
> (SFA, 22)

For all their lustre and their elaboration these poems present a morality of struggle and action. And for a poet who, as Jane Mayhall has noted, embraced "the values of the tentative,"[5] Garrigue came increasingly to value action through the performance of healing acts. One of her final poems, "After Reading *The Country of the Pointed Firs*" (*SFA*, 19–20) presents a woman resembling Garrigue's actress figures who also must resist despair and take action to express faith. Through the outlines of Sarah Orne Jewett's 1896 novel, she elaborates upon a vision in which a woman lives heroically in an order of civil exchange with her neighbors.

The reasons for this poet's attraction to the Jewett novel may appear obvious. Garrigue's own novella, *The Animal Hotel* (1966), although a beast fable, presents a woodland matriarchy in which animals reveal a nurturing interdependency as the central character gradually unfolds her hidden past. The qualities of Jewett's sixty-seven-year-old Mrs. Todd must have been deeply attractive to Garrigue, for her strength resembles the quality this poet cultivated in her depiction of women in poems and fiction. As Jewett wrote of her character:

> It is not often given in a noisy world to come to the places of great grief and silence. An absolute archaic grief possessed this countrywoman; she seemed like a renewal of some historic soul, with her sorrows and the remoteness of a daily life busied with rustic simplicities and the scents of primeval herbs.[6]

In Garrigue's poem a woman, although mourning, must create her own "doses." While grief and loss haunt the woman, she takes from the woodland itself and from her garden her sources of power: healing herbs. The poem's form underscores the central character's connective, therapeutic actions through its girding of alliterative effects and assonance, its compounds and vigorous use of the vernacular. In this personified realm crows "liked to walk", there's "a town of birds," bees "go when they could to the wood," and "wind walked on the roof like a boy." The woman makes intimates of even nonhuman elements. Repetitions of the conjunction "and," over thirty repetitions of the conjunction in all, reinforce our sense of the woman's search for connection. Through neighborly kindnesses, and through the plants she searches out, the woman, like Garrigue's performers, must fashion a way of life from disciplined action:

> And she had knitting and folks to visit,
> Preserves to make, and cream tartar biscuit,
> She knew where was elocamp, coltsfoot, lobelia,
> And she'd make a good mess up for all as could use it,
> And go to the well and let down the bucket
> And see the sky there and herself in it
> As the wind threw itself about in the bushes and shouted
> And another day fresh as a cedar started.
>
> (SFA, 20)

This sense of community oscillates with isolation just as "change and loss" resonate. A woman "with a well not near and a barn too far / And the fields ledgy and full of stones" (SFA, 19) offers homemade heroics, overcoming as do so many of this poet's female performers an inhospitable climate.

Performance as an act of aesthetic and spiritual affirmation is most fully rendered through the 213 lines of "Studies for an Actress," one of the most ambitious poems to explore creativity by an American woman. Garrigue illuminates strategies through which her central figure may reclaim the governance of her own plenitude. The actress has now become a figure who must more consciously grasp at her own resources; she studies her self-accounts. "Studies for an Actress" expresses the actress's vacillations, "caught now in her alternatings / Before the incessant intervenings" (SFA, 5). She would reconstruct the net of spiritual and emotional correspondences that allows her to artfully perceive and in consequence to artfully perform. Of her work, Garrigue had said that she hoped "to justify . . . infatuation with sensation, pleasure, appearance, by making the object perenially accessible to, perennially violent, magnetic, bristling with the *activities and ambivalences* of insight" [emphasis mine] (TSP, 85). As Laurence Lieberman has suggested, through the *performance* of her despair the actress comes closest to being healed.[7] Yet "Studies for an Actress" is neither an exorcism nor a purification of the actress's desires; "ambivalences of insight" remain charged. As in the moments when we are first introduced to her, the actress must trade in riches. She must again find that "her heart [has] grown richer by this peril met" (SFA, 2).

Inspired by the 1959 Dubrovnik performances of the opera singer Galina Vishnevskaya, "Studies for an Actress" is organized primarily through the process of questioning the nature of

the creative process. The actress is estranged from her own ability either to experience her life creatively or to act. "A cloudy
counterfeiting takes her up, / Imbroglio of play to which she's
card" (SFA, 2). The actress, tellingly, wishes to become other
selves, each an "odd she":

> . . . she believes her differing masks hide no one
> But what the action brought her to be
> As if they were a foreign element
> That she put on and then put off,
> Performing in them alien acts,
> The I that was another, that odd she.
>
> (SFA, 4)

"Alien acts," "that odd she": such phrases suggest "The Stranger." Most clearly action creates the self; the self is not prior to its
action. Garrigue not only suggests an existentialist stance for her
actress but the ability to recast identity. She assumes the power of
the other—to be alien. The assumption of strangeness exhilarates
and offers intimations of unknown orders to both the actress and
her audience.

Figures from the collective unconscious both inform and
threaten creativity by their "large, impersonal strength." Through
them Garrigue reveals both the artist's anxiety and her sense of
trespass. "Assailed by knowledge of a plenitude," she is haunted
by her perception of the largeness of response that they demand
of her. The demonstratives "this" and "that" point up the very
nonspecificity of the act these figures seek:

> She flees all action now, she has gone in
> Upon a demi-day that sinks towards night
> Under instruction from the strangest powers
> She would appease and cannot, who reveal
> In the most obscure and sinking down of ways
> This that they want which will fulfill
> That which she does not know, which she must do.
> Can she turn back? The path is overgrown.
> Ahead,
> Roads like lines in the palms of the hand
> Now fade.
>
> (2–3)

Like the performer of "Opera of the Heart," the actress tem-
porarily withdraws, for the gods have grown into full-scale

taskmasters whom she cannot appease. They are the "strangest powers." "Players of the immense," they perform upon a scale that threatens by its very enormity. Other godlike presences similarly compel her:

> Garbed figures, rapt and wrought
> All to one aim and ending, blazonries
> Like constellations of a zodiac
> She pulls against and yet is driven by,
> And she would ask these players of the immense
> Pardon for her fitfulness.
>
> (SFA, 4)

Like "the stranger" they would have this central figure convey alien modes of being and knowledge.

Significantly, the actress's loss of power is linked with a fall from a net, a fall that has been developed through web-spinning language and near language ("the shuttling flux" rather than "the shuttling flax"). Only a relational netlike force permits her to perform. Otherwise, there is "nothing to hold her back from this descent / Into a void, opaque, unlit, / When out from feeling, cut the links." Nets emerge as display and linkage. It is, however, "Indifferent death" who extracts the "binding element" from the actress. Her enemy is the "prince of shades," a death figure who would remove her from the stage. The actress's urgency is compelled by her increasing sense of mortality. Like the woman at the center of "After Reading *The Country of the Pointed Firs*" she must "knit herself" within a world of performing actions if she is to defeat mortality.

The poem modulates into tones of supplication. As Helen Vendler reminds us, "Lyric has, historically, voiced a prayer or a complaint, both presupposing a listener, the 'thou' of remedy."[8] The actress who performed the part of Faith (faith in an artistic vision and a quality of active, form-conscious perception) now no longer perches upon a balcony but places herself among the natural and the specific: "valerian, dianthus columbine," the living and the evanescent succeed beyond the "godded bull" and the "stone lips." The movement into nature prefigures the actress's acceptance of change; she acts her way into the natural world composed of time that, she discovers, mirrors her own fluctuating nature. She "prays to pray, but cannot start" and "recommends" to the light the release of the self's hive: "That clamor of the throng of voices / Kept down, locked in, but murmurous as bees / Ready as ever for the nuptial flight, . . ." (SFA, 7). The actress has rehearsed an array of attitudes, and now the release of the voices as "nuptial flight" meshes the poem's bridal imagery; her bride is her poet-actress and the nuptial flight is the wedding of opposites that the poem makes possible.

In the final stanza the actress, as mistress of voices, prays to fully embody creativity. At last, the nuptials of the "prince of shades" metamorphose into another sort of bridal feast altogether: the marriage of the self's swarming voices:

> She prays if nothing else to be
> In some dissolving medium of light,
> A pond that's set to catch the arrowy beams,
> Reflective and obedient as that.
> She prays then to change
> If it's in changing that things find repose.
> She prays to praise. She prays to be
> Condensed now to one desire
> As if it were very life performing her.
>
> (7–8)

We are left with the image of the creative self as a pond reflecting light, an image that is actively receptive. The actress would be "one desire" compelled by "the throng of voices" and united with the life energy itself. As we shall see in her poems organized around "water walks," the image duplicates Garrigue's emphasis on flux. The actress prays "to change / If it's in changing that things find repose." Her acceptance may break despair's hold; by moving from the static to the motile, the actress realizes that in change the self follows its essential temporal nature and as such may naturally realize its power. Her final prayer is then both to condense and reunify the self with the force of life, "as if it were very life performing her." The artist becomes not simply a conduit for life but part of the lifestream itself. The poem articulates art as dynamic selfhood; the artist is "performed" as much as she "performs." As Lieberman has it, "Life must be *performed* to be life . . . and performed 'at breakneck speed of remorse' if it is to keep up with the very timetable of survival."[9] The mask becomes urgent and valid, a cluster of "selves" transfigured.

While Garrigue has moved a good deal from "The Stranger," in both poems the abilities to perceive and accomplish action are initially frustrated. Both poems concern women who create, one "out of sorrow," the latter a mature artist who creates as part of an articulation of her varied identities and as a recognition of her desire to perform. Both poems play upon subversions of failure; women artists failing to meet their desires nevertheless compose from loss the poem or performance as "other." Pointedly each woman, "an odd she," may be so both to herself and to her audience.

Among the many drafts of "Studies for an Actress" a note indicates the poem's importance for this poet: "I lived for certain grandeurs that fade fast"—me, JG" (Berg). As the past tense and the initials asserting authorship suggest, the note is to be read as a self-assessment. By signing her note, this poet makes clear that she is engaged in a self-accounting. The note is particularly illuminating for understanding her experience of her own processes: desire may be constant but the nature of vision ever fitful. The poet's studies may then most ambitiously concentrate on vacillation in the inspiration itself. The artist's life is composed of both "grandeurs" and failures as the creative vision fluctuates. The very transcience of the creative moment is repeatedly examined among her notes: "[T]he secret is gathered together only an instant and an instant after, there is the withdrawing, the ebbing of that secret life back into the indestructible parts" (Berg). The recording of such moments sustained her, as an undated note makes clear: "The truth is that I live as much as ever a step away from the brink. My only salvation is in moments; by actions of perception and redemption" (Berg). The lyric moment had been of crucial importance. The sensibility of self-consciously female speakers and female performers that she explored in "The Stranger" compels her poems that illuminate creativity. A poet is not simply one "odd she," but many. If she suffers she may nevertheless make "a stately thing." And it is through attempting "actions of perception and redemption" that she may regain her power.

3
THREATENING ROMANCE
The Subversive Heart

The heart is Garrigue's subversive organ. A pursuit of "the dissi-
dent structure of happiness" through explorations of the
affections, she suggests, remains hazardous. It may be only in
departing one another that we evade our own ignorance: "It is in
the poignancy of tests / That we strike fire at the source, / At
farewell that we clasp what we know, . . ." (*SFA*, 73). And while
sexual love prompts the imagination, imagination may outdis-
tance love, "fattening" on the lover. "To die on him is not to dye
the dark," Garrigue writes in an uncanny, masquelike poem.
("Dialoque à Quatre," *MR*, 34). Her Renaissance pun on orgasm
couldn't be more explicit; sexual love with the concommittant
possibility for women of traditional domestic arrangements and
their requirements on energy and independence may not feed
anyone's muse enough. Yet for a poet committed to her art,
romance itself may be threatened by art. And Garrigue takes
curious pleasure in threatening romance through her descriptions of the transforming pressures of a restless imagination.
    Garrigue's love poems are among her most demanding, for she
herself felt particularly challenged by the conventions of romantic love. "How can we forget the ambivalences we are heir to"
(Berg), she wrote among her notes. Perhaps nowhere is ambivalence stronger in this work than in her investigations of
romance. In 1965 Stephen Stepanchev was already noting that *A
Monument Rose* was in large measure testing "the limits of ro-
manticism."[1] The powers of imagination and the powers of romantic love alternately conflict or merge; finally, if one must arise
victorious it is the imagination, for the imagination creates and
elaborates upon romantic passion. The heart itself is divided
between the natural and the artificial, between instinctual and
learned responses.
    Garrigue's fascination with images of romance emerged in her

childhood. An unpublished account—a draft for a biographical
sketch—reveals her early fascination with romantic inflation.
She reflects on "artful" images of romance:

> Alas, as a child I was misled by two steel engravings. . . . In the first
> you had a barque and two sleeping lovers he upon her breast in the
> full savor of that sweet exhaustion which comes as a final requital to a
> good deal of energetic ardor. It is a gilded barque, scalloped and shell
> like, and well may the lovers sleep in their gilded Grecian voiles and
> vales and filets round the head and curls and flushed cheeks, for a
> small naked spirit drives them over a milky sea. The horsepower
> being that of two amiable lusty dolphins with sea-weed for reins. Of
> the other, they are awake, the lovers, a silken sail bellies out and
> Amour holds lines coiled gracefully around the necks of two power-
> ful swans. She looks up to him in all the puissance of female languor
> before surrender and he, curls trailing his forehead, stares down at
> her. Enticing. Seduction and its rewards thereafter. Tell me no more.
> I, indeed, was told all. Thus did I believe the world prospered. (Berg)

Such engravings, of course, do not constitute "the world." Se-
duction may not be followed by "rewards thereafter." In turn, her
poems reveal the heights of the high romantic imagination just
before it discovers its own errors. Our absolute longings for
romance may defeat intimacy; we may idealize too readily and
depart from one another too hurriedly.

Garrigue's earliest published poems, appearing in 1938 while
she was a student at the University of Chicago, concentrate on
love in ways that anticipate her later preoccupations. She makes
the male persona of "Boy's Resume at Twenty-Three" complain
that he is neither bright nor handsome, his only possession being
love.[2] "Clark Street" with its brightly lit decay is a forerunner to
"The Circle" from Garrigue's introductory work through New
Directions: "Clark Street, like a sudden mushroom, / After six
blooms gold and scarlet."[3] In these early poems she focuses upon
tableaus suggestive of her later calibrations: a predominance of
luxuriant color and the image of love as a youthful figure so
"tensile in his purity he might / Arise . . . , birdfooted like a
god."[4] They reveal her tendency toward wry investigation of the
romantic. If women were culturally to be held in the confines of
romance, already she was determined to apply pressures to convention.

In a 1947 essay, "The Heart and the Lyre," Louise Bogan wrote
of a place for contemporary women in poetry, attempting to

include women within a tradition that largely excluded them, particularly within the politics of compiling anthologies.

> Though she may never compose an epic or a tragic drama in five acts, the woman poet has her singular role and precious destiny. And, at the moment, in a time lacking in truth and certainty and filled with anguish and despair, no woman should be shamefaced in attempting to give back to the world, through her work, a portion of its lost heart.[5]

While Bogan's essay provides women with a role, the role is one in which the more limited concerns of the single, isolated heart are their territory, a preserve from which women, the implication seems apparent, are perhaps not fully equipped by nature to leave. Ambitiously, Garrigue had reflected from the start of her career on public themes, questioning national celebrations after the United States' victory over Japan, recording anti-Semitism, seeking a variety of Yeatsian transcendence and sacramental radiance within the ordinary. Similarly, in her poems on the heart, the heart is a more powerful organ for arriving at new measures of both thinking and feeling than was superficially conceived to be women's traditional focus. In turn, "a portion of [the times'] lost heart" is more often reflected upon than returned intact within Garrigue's poems. Love is "that top to wind" (CWM, 43) she would write in midcareer. While she is a "celebrant" of romantic love, most often she is an ironic explorer who over-whelms cultural equations.

One of her earliest poems of the 1940s, "The Clovers," reveals concerns that Garrigue articulates throughout the heart motif; the affections as a source of paradox, the heart as "willing and unwilling, ignorant and imitator" as "woodland," an image of constriction, and as "flood," an image of excess. She composes a catalogue of oppositions between the natural and the unnatural, the visible and the invisible, wish and will, imitation and igno-rance, multiplicity and singularity, surface and depth. The heart is a divided organ, self-subverting and a source of quarrels. Not simply a province of emotions, the heart serves as her localized site in which thinking and feeling, the artificial and the natural, meet:

> For the heart, willing and not willing,
> Is glassed under as clover in a stand of storm water.
> In the downy sink of the ground
> Rain is an inch deep over the heads of those four leaves

And the sides turn silver in the embossed
Pond-meadow. Think of a whole army of clover
Hidden under, lace all, green as an apple.

For the heart, willing and not willing,
Stands in a rain-settle too, transparent
To all in a vale, where the firm skin of wish
Dapples and lines it
And its veins are exposed, pale
To the tremble of world's rage, ail.
But not sky is reflected nor sun from the gray pall of
    heaven,
Not seed whistling by nor bird dipping.

Transparency has its savior, visible and invisible!
For as the clover stem suggests no relation
To its top parent, and under that water
Leaves stay in a stitching, sewn like a cobbled silk,
So the heart, as obscurely rooted
Is as rooted, though with a pretty way
It lies in the film of flesh, a marrow of constancy.

But nor sun reaches to nor strenthens by air
That fond delicacy
And the dwarf hidden roots, apparent to none,
Obstruct the dark muscle, a clarity upside
But a dark land thereunder.
Willing and unwilling, ignorant and imitator,
In the source of that woodland, the improvident flood.

(N&SP, 8)

Significantly, the clovers are placed in the rhetorical field of
embroidery; the heart is presented in juxtaposition to the artfully
conceived clovers. Metaphors of ornamental stitchery or artful
display predominate. As if in a display case, the clovers are
"glassed under." A number of terms refer to fabric and as such
suggest costume: "lace," "Leaves stay in a stitching / Sewn like
cobbled silk." The "pond-meadow" is "embossed." Here "the
firm skin of wish / Dapples and lines." The sky is a "pall," a
cloaking overspread. The heart itself is only "transparent / To all
in a vale"; in Garrigue's pun, through a vale or a special "veil" of
second sight, the heart is curiously wrought and continuously
doubled. As such, by calling attention to artifice, the poet directs
us to her own artistry, the act of remaking the heart. Her strategy
is self-conscious. She is a woman writing of the heart, a tradi-

tional province for women, and in turn she employs ornament terms commonly associated with women. Yet this poet subverts the limitations ascribed to the heart; her heart is as powerful as a mind.

As her language dramatizes a quarrel, we are led to Garrigue's "dark land thereunder": "the clover stem suggests no relation / To its top parent." Each root of the heart is a "dwarf," as if subverting the "upside" of "clarity." Contradictory doubles run throughout the poem, particularly in its final lines, chains of paradox that do not collapse difference: "Willing, unwilling, ignorant and imitator, / In the source of that woodland, the improvident flood." She completes her paradoxical equation through syntactic and semantic reversals and the upending of scale and density.

More than twenty years later among the new poems in *New and Selected Poems*, Garrigue again locates the heart against a background of stitchery, here in "An Improviation Upon the Theme of the Lady and the Unicorn" (*N&SP*, 128–30). She improvises and elaborates upon the richly figured tapestries in Paris:

> We are held by the heart as he hands it
> Not to be played with or eaten by his lady.
>
> . . . .
> The bather bathes in the parapets of lilies,
> And earth bears everywhere the upstanding flower,
> Fruit wood with yellow quince clearly,
> Clearly in a fresh candor conceived.
> The vair-rose trumpet that her Michael blows,
> He jams the dragon to its knees,
> And the small heart sparkles amidst the leaves
> Of the one thousand flowers, and flares.
>
> (*N&SP*, 130)

The heart "flares" amid stitching's multiplicity—self-defined and complete, yet its existence ever a temptation to destructive energies. Is the woman tempted to play with the heart or consume it? In the earlier "Gravepiece" (*MR*, 20) the heart is in turn about to be consumed until the speaker becomes the heart's rescuer: "the heart . . . [has been] pried from the worm's small jaws" in this macabre poem that reflects Garrigue's fascination with imagery of the heart—a fascination that continued throughout her career.

Lovers in her earliest poems attempt to create a connection with the natural world yet may discover their very divisiveness

from nature. Division, in fact, was one of Garrigue's first themes.
Countering images of artifice are those poems in which nature
becomes a lover or in which lovers identify with nature. Landscapes are frequently fleshy, as if lover and land are momentarily
one and the same; by conflating land and flesh she suggests that
the poet seeks a continuum between herself and the natural
world. In "Invocation to Old Windylocks" (MR, 30–33), for instance, a mountain is envisioned as a giant woman, and the
poem becomes an erotic embodiment.

> Night birth of cloud, to be
> In the delirium of mists or thy clear sea—
> Diamond cast forth from the earth's rage,
> Rarified arrogance beside whom
> The clear star rests and reigns,
> Deep in the midsummer casque of flesh
> Exalted, secret, calm, and vast, to stay—
>
> Into which the night clambers and the day—
> Thicket entangled, up which in ropy ascent
> Vapors in the clear fervors of morning rest
> Like a mid-Norway
>
> And me held to thee, infatuate on thy flank
> Great prow, aërial bulk—
> Florilegium, stepping forth into fresh-running light—
> Arcana coelestia . . .

The speaker would hold to and ride this eroticized form into
"fresh-running light." "The Land We Did Not Know" (WW, 73)
similarly reveals the self as a tactile explorer of nature-as-lover,
this poet's frequent use of questions underscoring her endeavor
to understand exigencies:

> And thus, my upland slope, I touch you here
> With fabulous endeavor, like someone who comes
> To greet you, walking on the tiptops of the trees.

Images of the natural world dominate the only poem of her
own that Garrigue intended to include within the anthology of
love poems she was editing in the months before her death.
(Nancy Sullivan, editing the collection after Garrigue died, introduced sections of the book with Garrigue's lines and added
additional poems by Garrigue.) "Incantatory Poem" explicitly

connects love to nature, art, and transfiguration; the poem is as
much about making images as about readying the self for a lover:

> I make a poem I shape upon a prayer
> To my unfathered child, dark come to flower,
> And shaping pray love brings
> Where we will lie,
> Crossed with birds out of your name
> I stole by watches of the griefless dream
> In the lament of the wine-transfiguring world.
>
> (WW, 87)

Here is a realm of transformation in which imagination and
emotional attachment coincide. The poem celebrates the female
lover as a fluent image-maker in control, as with her actress able
to create a "wending in between the gulfs, / That effort to create
the links" among the affections. Through near obsessive repetitions, composition is linked to a metaphoric pregnancy; the
poem emerges as both a product of love and a form of lover. The
speaker gives birth to language through naming her lover: "Your
name wearing water in cloud and flame" (WW, 86); "The world
bearing flowers out of your name" (WW, 87). The lover is simultaneously both her art and her "other." The word, "the name," is
continual birth; the "word" turns into Garrigue's infinite child.

Garrigue's poems of intimacy conceived through the image of
nature are countered by those in which she investigates romance
as a choice problematized by a commitment to art. Frequently
Garrigue's speakers choose to define themselves as "artful" lovers
or as women who must make a choice between art and love. As
Cheryl Walker has noted, both nineteenth- and twentieth-century
women poets write about conflicts between love and art[6] as they
face the "double bind" that Suzanne Juhasz described over ten
years ago: "Woman" and "poet" have long been considered "contradictory" identities.[7] In poems focusing on love, then, women
may write of the conflicted cultural status of love and art and
their own attempts to discover balance.

Garrigue's poetry revises the theme in which a woman focuses
upon her self-concept as an artist and her choice to define herself
principally through art. In particular, her poems reveal her ambivalence; sexual love may be a hazard to imaginative power yet
sexual love may, paradoxically, liberate the imagination; she
makes the poem itself an erotic other in terms traditionally re-

served for romance. *A Water Walk by Villa d'Este* opens with "The Hunt" (*WW*, 11–12) in which her speaker chooses art over eroticism. Sexual love "vanishes" once the "deed" is accomplished, whereas art "has no aim," remains "more constant," and offers an eroticized pleasure. In "I Sought from Love" (*WW*, 49–50), however, the poet in part reverses her earlier equation. The poem is located at almost the halfway point in *A Water Walk by Villa d'Este*, reflecting a progression in which love now creates art and as such contributes to self-actualizing.

Frequently, Garrigue merges art and love into artful romance. The diversion of the romantic woman or man is ceaseless elaboration upon the loved one. As such, let romance beware art, she suggests. If the specter of traditional heterosexual relationships threatened women's ability to make art she subverts the equation. The imagination's energy may be stronger than physical passion. The energy of ornamenting is perhaps most explicit in "The Mask and Knife" (*E&C*, 51), a love poem that nevertheless examines the threat the imagination bears to romance. The speaker would adorn her lover; she would have him "clad like dominoes / In every stripe and lozenge" in a search for "a gauged discord," paradoxically a measured and as such delightful disorder. Stevens-like in its richness of palette, Garrigue's poem links an erotics of imaginative dressing with an oblique bullying. The speaker is a contemporary Eurydice at the moment when Orpheus has turned to her and thus sent her back to the underworld: "The angels of your eyes are all my foes. / Now forward gaze nor deepward gaze no more // But backward gaze to gaze me into hell."

In a later version, which appeared in *New and Selected Poems* (17), the subtle Eurydice analogy has been replaced, as if it were an imposition upon the poem's structure. Expanded sea imagery moves the poem, without mythological allusions, toward integrity within its own terms. The later version's final line, "And your very name—its lips make weights in me," is taken from the earlier version's last quatrain. As the speaker would "weight" the loved one with colors, textures, and odors, her own restless imagistic energies create an icon of the loved one. Simply the lover's name would now "make weights" within her. The self may be solidified in such a development perhaps, but given the seascape of much of the poem, the self may more likely be sunk, harnessed by its own ornamentations. For all its color, this poem is an exercise in anxiety. The frivolity of this dressing with its lozenges and jellied colors descends to the speaker's "weighted" final line, as if the pressure of a more conventional metaphysic were about to sink its speaker.

Deities, as in so much of Garrigue's work, arise in poems that dramatize romantic desire. In love poems they may begin as soft-faced girls or boys before turning into statuary—a statuary to which Garrigue applies irony, disrupting appearances. Her ambivalence is reflected within such icons; they may be Medusas who, their own light cast upon themselves, are subject to destruction while "all this surrounds . . . like great stone." Her Daphnes may find "lust in . . . metamorphosis" or conversely turn monstrous for their refusal to meet their own Appollonian powers. Her lovers risk "imitat[ing] perfection in a void." She is attracted to conventional representations of love as a god or goddess. And yet such figures become hardened, ravaged, or penetrated by other presences; they succumb to time or diminishing passions. Garrigue exploits the conventions of courtly love—conventions that may have seemed attractive to her for their formality, decorum, and very appearance of granting artful attention to women. Yet her drama most energetically focuses upon the conventions' disruption. As late as the new poems within *New and Selected Poems*, in the ornate "Ballade" (146–50), Garrigue concentrates upon a masque revealing the court-ship between lovers who put on "the luminous body of new love." Similar to the web-captured figure in "A Dream," written during roughly the same period, lovers struggle within the bonds of their hearts. Contemporary versions of Venus and Mars, these lovers find "their senses roped" (*N&SP*, 48) until romance disintegrates, and the poem invokes the powers of absolution and the recovery of speech.

The longevity of romance is similarly contemplated in "Invitation to a Hay" (*N&SP*, 94–96). The poem presents an invented "natural world" in which the speaker's creation of fantasy allows her to imagine a haven for herself and her lover. Love in this fabulistic landscape may refine sensibilities:

> Aërial would we be
> With love's finest courtesies,
> By all that shapes of earth and air
> Can subtilize the senses with
> Until they have grown rapt
> On emanations of a light. . . .

                                                                (*N&SP*, 96)

After setting up a catalogue of sensual temptations the poem acknowledges its own illusory nature. The land itself is pointedly a sphere of rifts and breaks in which markings of civilization and nature intersect. Garrigue questions the province of fantasy even while she seems to recommend fantasy. "Endowment" only occurs "so long as we would stay" in this landscape amidst "ravines," and "broken towers." Her idyll is threatened by rebellion from within:

> My dear, and will you be
> Content to dwell with me
> Eating of illusion
> Daily and nightly?
>
> (96)

"Little Ballad" (151–52) provokes questions between lovers as well. Contemplating the future, a woman asks the Echo-like pertinent question: "And then?" Through nursery-rhyme-like rhythms she eerily puts to question the male's assertions. What seems initially to be courtship's joy may loom as psychic death, for the young man, like Narcissus preaching his own practice, wishes the woman to "look in / To that still place in the stream" (151). There the woman might be enthralled by her vision of herself; still waters reflect a "clear" image but a perverse one, for the self to Garrigue is more like rapidly running water, surely mobile. Beyond surfaces rise the fountainlike energies of identity. The woman is not so much a waif as a stern witness, for she knows change is ours whether we seek it or not: "What then? she cried, what then?" The woman's question reflects the curve of emotions in many of Garrigue's poems in which self and other, if briefly united, must submit to divisiveness over their futures.

What are Garrigue's final conceptions of romantic love? She emerges with a more immediate wedding between high rhetorical energies and more direct than usual accounts of the personal in Studies for an Actress. Like her giralda, she engages in "surveying her legends" (31). Love fails when it is not a form of artful discipline. The poems continue to bring the heart motif forward (there are over two dozen repetitions of the word "heart" in Studies alone). Lovers are cautioned to learn from one another, and there is much insistence on discovering joy in the face of loss. Wine is a secular drink, less of a sacramental intoxicant than in earlier volumes. Her familiar themes, commitment to self-growth and desire as inspiration, are more fully embodied. Yet the divine personifications of love that Garrigue had begun addressing in her earliest poems are now largely absent. There is "no walking in those gardens / In a ring of stone queens—/ Bertha Broadfoot, Geneviève—/ With Love at my side" (SFA, 32). The speaker berates herself, for the past has put her "out of use"; she cannot comfortably assume a romantic's mantle. Love is no longer the icon so much as the boy with the ephemerality of human dimensions. Notably in "Song for 'Buvez Les Vins du Postillon'—Advt." the lovers must be "drunk on the wines of the postillon" at, tellingly enough, the Hôtel du Départ (SFA, 37).

Such poems exemplify a change in perspective more than a reversal in thematic interest. Yet a sense of loss resonates through the late work. "Grenoble Café" (36) proves representative. Unlike most of Garrigue's poems that take love or lovers as their focus, "Grenoble Café" presents a realistic tableau before which the speaker is a spectator, able here to distance herself, a technique this poet has most often avoided in her love poems:

> At breakfast they are sober, subdued.
> It is early. They have not much to say
> Or with declamations fit only for whisper
> Keep under pressure the steam of their joy.
> She listens, usually. It is he who talks,
> Surrounding her with the furious smoke
> Of his looking that simply feeds,
> Perhaps, her slightly traveling-away dreams
> That, if you judge from her cheek,
> Young and incomparably unbroken,
> Are rich with the unknowning knowing
> Of what he has said the time before
> And with the smiles coming down from the corridor
> Of how it will be for year on year,
> Nights as they'll be in his rough arms.
>
> (SFA, 36)

Garrigue's preoccupation with the imagination and the mind's ability to idealize the other informs the poem. While the man attempts to feed upon her attention, the woman is richly engaged with her own imagination. Perhaps for the moment the woman may be more fully occupied with her imagination than with the actual man before her. The qualifiers "furious" and "rough" suggest the possibility of the woman being "broken" in the future.

The poem is as much about the power of imagination as the power of love.

In her final work this poet has, then, returned to one of her earliest questions; how might the poet reconcile her love and her poetry in a climate that diminishes both or relegates to women love alone as a proper sphere? In the late "Dialogue" (41), Garrigue reinvigorates the dialectic between love and art. A comic dog-as-artist transforms language, provoking us to note the capricious quality of words:

> Dreams, said the dog,
> Suffice us not.
> We strain at eels and catch a gnat instead.
> Who'll have Red Rabbit
> And his riding wood
> And my lady moon in a simpled hood?

A poem as a net, sacking, a web—recurrent images of creative form for Garrigue—makes immortality possible, the dog suggests. The cat's answer offers us the possibility that love for its "besetting property" may be the net of artistic creation, a creation not only of a child but of the poem. Although the poem is pointedly a dialogue, the female cat-as-artist has the last word:

> Said he,
> It all depends on a lasting net
> If you'd fish for eternity.
>
> Said she,
> Love's besetting property!

The net of art and the net of love unite as conceptions of immortality. Love is not referred to as having "ancient properties" as in "Invitation to a Hay" but a "besetting property"; love is her protean subversive.

A precarious merging is effected through her dialogues upon artful love. Pointedly, however, love's "besetting" qualities, the possibility of love's subversion of convention, its ability to unsettle established orders, most interests her. Not for her any final certainties between lovers. Issues of attachment are problematized, and desire itself becomes an independent force that disrupts convention.

In these love poems we discover Garrigue's emphasis on pleasure and sensation as these are in turn influenced by disruptive energies. In the following chapter I will explore her focus upon desire as movement; it is independence rather than attachment that dominates many of the poems discussed in this final chapter. As Jane Mayhall writes, Garrigue's "impetus was to overcome barriers, to eliminate conventional borders; and finally, among the dangerously deep levels of self, to transform, reinterpret, change."[8] Through her practice in flux she discovers a new authority within desire that transcends the romantic.

4

WATER WALKS
The Authority of Desire

Throughout Jean Garrigue's poetry desire has been prominent. Her emphasis on sight, for instance, dissolves barriers to desire. Her actress is defined in terms of her desires. The heart is characterized by both obstruction and excess, a "flood" of desire that overcomes boundaries. When at midcareer Garrigue began experimenting with poems that are organized around water walks—walks by water or walks in landscapes that assume the qualities of water—she explored desire and the mind's continuum with the natural world. Through these poems in particular she sought to identify herself with the transformative imagination as a discipline that acknowledges the strength of desire: the merging of "passion" and "want." The capacious forms of these poems offered her scope for exultance. Less often hierarchical than conjunctive, meaning accretes but is not assimilated into readily perceived end-points. The poems, among her longest and most complex, serve as a significant indication of her ambition. While many of her earlier poems are structured as quarrels, in later forms this poet achieves a sustained performance of association and an imagistic richness seldom paralleled among her contemporaries.

For this poet, water serves as an image of poetic inspiration, "the source of the fury" that invests the poet's active perception. As Alicia Ostriker notes, "Water for women poets becomes a key image in the representation of erotic gratification, evoking both bodily and emotional intimacies and standing for the dissolving of boundaries not only between self and lover but between lovers and nature."[1] Yet water for Garrigue suggests both momentary "erotic gratification" and the sudden renewal of desire through the fountainlike urgencies of the self. This element that suggests the dissolution of boundaries also suggests the dissolution of conventional mastery. Fountainlike desires contest an authority that relies upon a stable self.

Garrigue's 249-line "For the Fountains and Fountaineers of Villa d'Este" (*N&SP*, 64–72) reveals her subversion of traditional structures of authority. She not only tests her ability to create an aesthetic structure of magnitude but, more importantly, asserts her acceptance of a desirous self who contests conventions of mastery. Each a "scandal of pleasure" (64), the fountains serve as metaphors for the intractability of identity and language. Like fountain waters, the seeking self is both self-spending and self-renewing through the energy of its desire. She offers practice in flux through her displays of language as play, the "down play and up play" and "play by water / And play by light on the water." Her "spectacle of waters" emerges as self-spectacle:

> Say that these are the fireworks of water,
> One hundred fountains on the tiers of plains,
> That goddesses enthroned hold spears of it,
> It erupts from the mouths of shagged eagles,
> And moss-legged gods, one side of the face worn off
>   by it,
> Straddle the silver, unmitigated flood.
>
>   (64)

Here, thirst mimics the fountain's volatility, for thirst

> . . . heaps on the brain,
> It plunges along the arm,
> In a sleep by leaves
> It buries half the blood.
> Taking one sinuous course down the breast
> It would thrust and lock round the heart in a trice.
>
>   (65)

From the brain to a "plunge" "along the arm," desire compels such writing; the fountains and the poets are each writers of sorts and in these moments of permeability might be "writing" one another. Garrigue competes with traditional notions of a stable creator as her own ceaselessly moving, restless lines emerge.

Through the one element of water, this poet suggests the interpenetrability of all elements within the natural world. She has departed from her image of fountains within her first book: "Who said our love must issue from / No cisterns of the ruddy sun / But like the artifice of fountains / Leap from cold, infertile sources" (*TSP*, 89). Water is now pointedly fertile and simultaneously creates earth forms: "vines" and "wreaths" of water, "water roots,

tentacles." Water unites with fire in another sort of "water burning"; the fountains form "fireworks," "burst rockets, "wet dusts,"
"furnaces." Each form "smoulder[s]." By uniting fountain waters
with other elements, this poet asserts the dominance of a mutable self, turning to both one of its gods and, in a quick shimmy
down the chain of being, originary life forms of lichen or fern:

> I am dank as a river god.
> Scallop on scallop of the primeval flat water leaf
> With no roots but in water, taking its substance from
>   liquid,
> Coats me and jackets me over.
> I am dense as lichen,
> Primordial as fern, . . .

> (N&SP, 66)

In a new approach, her speaker in the poem's second section
directly addresses the fountains, a strategy that makes the flux of
waters serve as a model for the speaker's desire. She pleas to be
endowed with a plenitude of being:

> Bequeath me, be with me, endow my hunger
> With sweet animal nature,
> Knit me in the plumes and the wands of your favor,
> Get me great vistas, jade-milky streams
> Where the source of the fury starts,
> Winking up the last supper of light.
> Get me chrysanthemums, great bulky heads,
> And a stem narrow as mercury
> Fit to support a bluet.
> And out of the reflections of water on stone
> Let me count the great arcs,
> The clusters rounded as grapes
> Or staccato as needles,
> All that momentum kept firm
> Propelled by the dry force of form—
> To rest, momentarily at least
> In the cataract of time—
> Leaves for his feathers on the breast of an eagle,
> Deep light of the long nights and years!

> (N&SP, 69–70)

She would seek connection and excess—"great bulky heads, /
And a stem narrow as a mercury. . . ." Time itself is a "cataract"—in the element of time she would achieve rest; as with her

actress, motility is the lyric poet's element and yet offers, paradoxically, repose. It is our effort to withstand time, she suggests,
that leads to our exhaustion. She seeks, then, knowledge through
movement in time: "I know of no fury that tells / More to me,
deafening, than that / Of a velocity past which I'd know / Nothing
but the hurl and fall" (N&SP, 65) Garrigue immerses herself in
transformation, seeking interpretation of both the fountains and
by extension her own multiple nature. Triple interpretation, tri-
ple-think, turns essential: "But you must thrice interpret to tell /
What is said by a flower in a spell, / Ascending the steps to the
gods . . ." Gradually, the speaker stands before her gods. If we
first must "descend by these paths, these perspectives" (70), we
now, in a kinetic echo of fountain movement, must be "ascending
. . . to the gods (71).

The artistry of the fountaineers has directed the inchoate element of water into form, yet water itself wears away the artfully
created gods. Paradoxically, the gods—emblems of perfection—
must bear the diminishments of flux. She may attain access but
not residence with her gods. She may momentarily "ascend," yet
her position in time requires her to continue within the motile
element of desire. The speaker is "sheathed in a grotto" (N&SP,
65) on the other side of this "shield of the water" (66). Yet her
"shield" erects "spears of water" (66), "the sword of a watery
swirl" (67). The speaker is "flailed to earth" (66) like the waters
themselves in her search for a cleansing consciousness. The
waters project, in Garrigue's insistence on an originary rebirth,
"the wild mists of forgetfulness" (68); through their energies even
memory may be cleansed, and the poet's shape-changing activity
may be reinvigorated. As such, this poet suggests that one may be
other than one singular self, experiencing the euphoric power to
alter not only experience but identity. She does not seek a consistent sense of selfhood but a more dramatic multiplicity of being,
for she has "gone the ways of each sense" (72) to take pleasure in
the velocity of her own metamorphoses.

In many of the poems we have examined, Garrigue's godlike
presences exist in a timeless sphere, impervious and critical of
the poet in flux. Garrigue's fountain figures, representatives of her
gods, however, are abraded. Here even the gods cannot control
origins or ends. A god hosts a "beardful of weeds," and the face
of one of the first we meet is eroded. Garrigue symbolically
cracks the fountain figures as godly symbols, challenging an
expected metaphysic in which gods remain impervious. The
speaker may be "flailed," yet she advances to the site of her

fountain gods to assert the power of her own desires and as such her own authority.

Significantly, Garrigue holds an ambiguous contest with gods, for godhead, she believed, may ultimately endanger the poet's voice. Obedience to a concept of immortals, self-consistent, may be antithetical to the fluctuating power that the lyric poet must assume through her awareness of desire. Nevertheless, a concept of godhead compelled this poet. She found in its expression a measure of her own value: "who loves his pain denies his god" (WW, 40) The gods offered her the opportunity to assert the strength of her own sensibility; an inarticulable and compelling force presented her with yet another place against which to enact conflict. Such conflict, in turn, generates the poems.

Garrigue's assessment of one of her contemporaries illuminates this issue. In her review she discusses Emily Dickinson's struggles with the idea of paradise. Garrigue's comments reveal her sense of the struggle she enacts with her own paradisal gods: "Emily Dickinson, who came out of a society that had taken the possibility of heaven seriously, worried it like a bone, mocked it, rejected it, yet could never escape intense preoccupation with the idea." She added that the poet under review's "all-acceptance seems all too easy."[2] In her own cosmology she never quite makes peace with otherworldly paradisal forces, whether symbolized by fountain figures of gods or dream figures who mock her actress's oscillations in such a late poem as "Studies for an Actress." Through the process of contending with images of omniscience, serenity, and perfection she escapes silence, that most pernicious of all punishments from the duplicitous gods who govern, she believed, the writer's psyche.

By its final stanza the fountain sequence modulates into an image of the gods' serenity. The poem's quiet end effects a stand-off. Tranquil and self-contained as the gods may be, the speaker's own stance is informed by her precarious human achievement that the gods, sealed in their completion, cannot fully know. Her triumph is to assume the authority of desire, "Passion" and "Want":

> Passion stares into their empty eyes
> Want sees the calm sweet water coursing,
> Artfully held in their mouths and pulsing,
> Blind waters tranquilly stemming there.
>
> (N&SP, 72)

Occasionally the poet may have wished for a calmly conceived art, but here she reaffirms a more unsettling vision. The final lines merge metaphorical surfaces to evoke the power of imagination and the self-spending elements of artistry. And yet Garrigue also calls up an image of the gods as "absentees" of desire; their eyes are now "empty," the waters themselves are "blind." Power rests in the mortal speaker who must support the full consequences of vision. It is the speaker's "passion" and "want" that survey the gods. The speaker is set off against the gods' placid indifference, for the fountains call up the speaker's desire to artfully perceive all that she may. Just as the fountains are intractable and capricious, so too must the poet's language inevitably behave. As Luce Irigaray writes, "fluid is always in a relation of excess or lack vis-à-vis unity," foregoing "any definite identification."[3] The remarkable volatility of fountains opposes unity, for water must destroy the fountain gods, wearing away their structures. Excessive, waters disrupt even as they display themselves. The poet's own authority is achieved through similar sensual energies; she presents us with an "alternative authority"—that of desire. As Ostriker points out, images of water in women's poetry serve to exemplify women's "alternative vision":

> Women poets who make the same plunge [into water] also evoke the dangerous and the mysterious, but they tend at the same time to evoke a sense of trust. . . . [T]he image of water comes to mean security instead of dread. It is alien, and yet it is home, where one will not be hurt.[4]

By now, the speaker who marvels at the fountains of Villa d'Este may seem familiar. She revolts against limitation, and yet she prizes limitation as an opportunity to test her own powers. She assumes a plenitudinous self, discovering in waters the flux that mirrors her own motile identity. In poems that focus even more closely upon the act of walking itself, the image of the walker may embody ambitious transformation. By writing of a persona in movement, this poet makes the act of seeking generously contemplative. She places herself "at the sweet borders of chance"; the opportunity to heighten desire rather than to master and possess animates these poems.

A short story of Garrigue's illuminates her sense of the consequences of refusing the changes that she associated with desire. "The Other One" refers to the second face of Rosemary Bastone, a distorted face concealed by a superficially charming

one. Behind a grown woman's facade of girlishness, Garrigue
discovers stunted development. As in Garrigue's other stories of
women passionately involved with one another in a richly multi-
valent female world, women come to one another for understanding. Yet refusing self-knowledge, Rosemary Bastone turns to
the narrator's prying, obsessive Aunt Mimi, whose attempts at
psychology cheapen this contemporary Daphne's struggle within
a "vegetal" light:

> The blight, the blight, of never changing, of so resisting change that
> resistance becomes that captivity, where all that one has not been is
> haunted, is killed, is bled invisibly, with constancy, by all that one is
> but should not be. Thus in the effort to avoid pain one has created
> more pain. Thus in the effort to avert change one creates a ghastly
> change. The fear of being human, the fear of moving with life, thus
> creating this monstrosity that dies between two worlds.[5]

A static hybrid, unable to metamorphose into a Venus, a figure
of artistic potency for Garrigue, Rosemary Bastone inspires mys-
tification rather than love. At the story's conclusion, Rosemary
Bastone returns to the arms of her mother, evading her own
growth. Garrigue's note in her unpublished novel further underscores her view of change:

> "It is the desire to postulate the absolute that murders us. We resist
> our changes and deny our growth in the feverish desire to hang on to
> a security." (Berg)

Her European travels and her writing influenced by travel
provided Garrigue with encounters that could not allow her to
"hang on to a security." A Water Walk by Villa d'Este and Country Without Maps are concerned with her intermittent European
travels. Her books present travel as a means of enlarging a sense
of self and practicing flux. The poems from these collections are
more direct and accessible than those of previous volumes; she
would open the network of the poem to write of expanded insight through travel. At the same time she would loosen her
metrics. The poems may begin with a formal pattern and later
subtly depart from that pattern into new extensions of language.
Circuitous movements are prevalent. Fountains do not transcend
their sources but return to their sources to ascend again. The
walker returns as well to her place of origin; a walk implies
return.

What are the implications of Garrigue's choice to focus upon such acts of recurrence? As she returns to motifs, so too she conceives of knowledge as a return, a circling back and then once again setting forth that deepens awareness through each cycle. In this context "Pays Perdu" (N&SP, 110–122), an unusual poem in Garrigue's body of work, proves revealing. She had not done anything in preceding volumes quite like it, nor would she repeat her experiment afterwards: lyric intermixed with prose paragraphs and a catalogue grounded by Blakean "minute discriminations": donkey tracks, scrub oak, "limestone dust," "the death's head grin of spurned headlands," a man "With the stub of a burnt-out cigarette / In the corner of his mouth like a sore." Significantly, in her introductory essay to her first collection Garrigue chose to discuss a hill as her hypothetical example of the poet's imagistic subject. Her mountain walk carries the image of creative search to culmination.

In this walk poem Garrigue enacts a search for creative authority, for here is a journey for the woman artist to her poem. "A Poem is a Walk," A. R. Ammons has titled one of his essays, for to Ammons a walk is "the externalization of an interior seeking."[6] As he points out, "a walk involves the whole person; it is not reproducible; its shape occurs, unfolds; it has a motion characteristic of the walker."[7] If we take Ammons's concept of the walk as an "externalization of an interior seeking," Garrigue's search for a lost village mirrors her search for creative authority. Creative authority arises as a journey to a part of the self that appears lost to time and yet intimates a sense of the psychological structures of the individual and her society. The poet must discover her sources of creativity partially outside a tradition with both its potentially oppressive strictures of institutionally-defined perfection and its potentially exhilarating structures of achievements. The poet must acknowledge the strength of her own "thirst." As in Garrigue's fountain sequence, "Pays Perdu" explores desire through the metaphor of thirst—physical thirst during a hot and tiring walk and thirst for insight at the center of the poem, the pays perdu, in which waters dominate, for water is the one element the villagers have "an abundance of." This is a place toward which thirst has been stimulated, where thirst eventually will be satisfied, and where the fluidity of landscape suggests the fluidity of language.

The poem opens with notes on form: "We are at rest strenuously / For all has form, moves with vivacious fluidity" (N&SP, 110). Through volatility, rest is possible; form resides within a paradox: "strenuous rest." The poem announces its own course: "something large, extensive" is about to occur. In Provence near the Var, the speaker and her friend, with the vaguest of directions, search for a mountain village linked to the outer world only by a donkey path.

Through their three-hour climb, as their path winds upward, downward, and again upward, they interrogate form, for form deceives throughout their walk. The act of seeing, as I have noted in the first chapter, is ever a test. Illusion dominates and, as in Marianne Moore's work, is rendered positive; Garrigue connects illusion to art—the chance of being deceived quickens into aesthetic pleasure. Illusion as an indication of the complexity of reference animates the poem. What seems near is far; a child at first thought to be mute at last speaks; a village in which the speaker and her friend had hoped to refresh themselves "disappears." Upon at last arriving at the village of Lacs, they discover that deception heightens; the village seems initially only to be a home for birds; a woman wears a man's cap and shoes; the full and the barren merge. In what ought to be a quaint, sleepy village, frenetic movement rules in a "delirium of birds" (N&SP, 117), and "bundles of hay kept flying past us on the backs of the man and woman . . ." (116).

As such, revision informs the poem. We and the speaker must revise our expectations as the rigors of the walk become rigors of perception, reflected in Garrigue's accretive syntax:

> And of the three-hour walk in the blaze of day
> Up the snail-spiralling way of the rough country—
> Scrub-oak and stone—
> And the three vertigoes when the path fell sheer
> By the cliffside straight to the river
> And there was white limestone dust and a chalky glare
> Blinding—
>   and the heat—till we cooked—
> And knew the beginnings of thirst—
>   and were lost
> Or deceived by a choice of paths. . . .
>
>   (N&SP, 112)

The breaking of the poem's form through dropped lines and frequent dashes is in part self-referential; the disruption in flow mimics not only a disruptive physical course but the uprush of the speaker's perceptions.

What she discovers is a village bearing its own marks of the
past but remaining connected to the contemporary world. For all
its suggestion of originative forces, its site near "the very birth of
a chaos," her village is grounded by the exigencies of time. While
the speaker and her friend had expected a *pays perdu* rather
romantically forgotten, they discover that a schoolteacher comes
for the one child, and a mailman, whether there's mail or not,
appears twice a week. Pointedly, the speaker's note that a mailbox
exists floats in white space as its own stanza:

> And we saw, going in, a bright blue postbox at
>   the side of his door.
>
> (*N&SP*, 117)

Here is discovery: the forgotten world is connected to the larger
world through, in a pun on "letters," language itself. Discovering
the village, the speaker discovers a precedent for the poet's authority. Her "country without maps" emerges as a psychic state
in which the poet may find strength through the paradox of both
volatile immersion in time and volatile instants of transcendence.

The speaker's decision to write to the village underscores Garrigue's conception of language as capricious and mobile form,
and the *pays perdu* as the imagination's country, accessible finally by means of desire for language. Through our desire for
language we may communicate with the most stubbornly mar-
ginal places within the psyche. As such, Garrigue insists on the
validity of her "forgotten country" as neither chimera nor
nostalgic daydream. Upsetting preconceptions and lively with
paradox, this region may appear only to those able to acknowledge their desires. She and her companion are compelled by
their desire for the village, a desire at first casual but later driven
by physical thirst and curiosity. Water and language merge, for
water, as she had written in her tribute to Dylan Thomas, is "the
dissembling element" (*WW*, 14). The speaker and her friend
imagine water before they discover it:

> And we dreamed up the café, for what town was without one,
> Where we would sit, steeped in mineral water.
> Citron pressé, and after that *café*
> Before we'd begin on water again.
>
> (*N&SP*, 114)

And at the village they find themselves enraptured with water:

> Then we rather crazy there at the tub, filling our hands
>   with water.
> And my friend lying prone and drinking from the pipe's
>   mouth. . .
> While bundles of hay kept flying past us on
>   the backs of the man and woman
>   and the one in a straw hat calling
> out to them in a language we had never heard to which
> was added the delirium of birds just before rain—
> swallows springing out of nowhere to shriek and to
> skirl and a swooping by pigeons while a battery
> of crows cawed by.

$$\text{(116–117)}$$

This walk, significantly, is a meditation on time. Just as Garrigue views the poem as a site that both records and takes place in time, she finds the village both a birthplace of form and a place struggling with the corrosive and regenerative powers of time. On the walk, however, time turns to oppressive and visibly scored weight: "History is time and it assailed us" (113). Still later, time is shown "grinding and pulverizing with an idiot's patience" (121). Garrigue "ascends into a past" made visible by the mountain's rough form. Time oppresses rather than inspires, for it appears unmediated by human consciousness. "To cut across time is the *imagination's* prerogative"[8] she wrote. Time without the measure of language, desire's element, oppresses consciousness.

The speaker's descent, cooled by rain, is marked by insubstantials that suggest the villagers' and the poet's strength despite adversity:

> And who was to say that their souls were held
> In the space here in between mountains
> As the thyme and the rosemary perfume the shadows
> That the great bodies cast down from their crowns?
> And who was to speak of mountain flowers
> That can blossom only after snow and deep frost,
> Their colors intensified by the rare air,
> Resisting the aridity, the cold nights, the poverty of
>   soil,
> Indeed, these very deprivations, that struggle
> Being necessary for their perfection of a few days?

It was not to say this
        in the great light
And the forms aloof over the serenity of ruins.

(*N&SP*, 122)

As Grace Schulman has remarked, "The initial confidence is
modulated to a tone of reverence for uncertainty and doubt. In
discovering the *pays perdu*, the poet has brought the lost self into
the light of consciousness."[9] The poem acknowledges the survival of a quality of attention that Garrigue defines as poetic: "a
struggle . . . for perfection of a few days."

"Pays Perdu" ends with a contemplation of both the shape of
thought—"'those intricate thoughts, those elaborate emotions'"—and a meeting with nature: "Where at the converging of
four peaks / A cloud makes a fifth" (122). Deceptively, the cloud
forms a peak like those of the mountains, although the cloud is,
of course, insubstantial and drifting. "[C]louds must indicate the
mountain's soul," Garrigue had written in the early "The Double
Praise that Simplifies the Heart" (*E&C*, 45). In "Pays Perdu" she
compels even the mountain's apparent stasis to be questioned.
The changes within a changing world receive as much authority
as the mountain, a traditional symbol of power and stability. She
grants authority to the fragrance of flowers and to a shifting cloud
through her annunciatory moments. She has successfully sub-
verted symbols of authority through symbols of evanescence and
shapeshifing. It is a project that she had begun in *The Monument
Rose*. That collection's title may in short form illustrate her project. Garrigue combines a traditional symbol of the ephemerality
of beauty with the monument, a symbol of lasting public re-
membrance, particularly that of men enaged in battle. As she
notes ironically in "Last Letter to the Scholar," "Forgive, because
I set up roses too / Improbable as madrigals" (*WM*, 41) for she
identifies the rose, a symbol so often associated with women and
passion, with the creative artist's highest powers.

Garrigue concludes her two final collections with walks in
which metaphors of fluidity are prominent. In these meditations,
spiritual presences and the energies of consciousness invest
landscapes: "A changeless changing, transforming into / An eth-
ereal storming, freshening, continuous" (*N&SP*, 167). Such walks
are a conscious effort to make explicit an unconscious design. In
"The Flux of Autumn" (*N&SP*, 166–68), the closing poem of *New
and Selected Poems*, Garrigue meditates upon a walker's continual surveying of her country without maps. Flux is explicitly

rendered as fluid; trees make "A sound as fierce as waterfalls", the ground is "leaf-rained," and spiritual voices are "mad as water hurled against a stone." The body's forward movement is the mind's movement, and in turn bodily movement unites land-scape with mind. Garrigue repeats some form of the word "walk" five times, a reminder that the woman consciously walks to release her own powers. "Misled by fevers then, by ditches lost, / By fireweed and the hawks that plunge" the woman must be informed by metamorphosis. Landscapes of consciousness are walked continuously as the mind discovers meaning:

> The clarity of mountains is obscured
> By what we'd fortify that must be dreamed.
> Old territory mapped and walked
> Nightly, daily, in the impetuous eye
> Of thought.
>   Until the dream's walked out.
>
>   (168)

Walking serves, then, as Garrigue's metaphor for the work of the imagination. Another meaning of the word *walk*, according to *Webster's*, is "to persist or recite hauntingly in the memory." One's inner dynamics are not "walked off" as if they were simply hallucinations but "walked out." The poet's landscape is "walked" into being. In a Dantesque scenario of leaves as "fire plagued spirits," this poet's self-haunting and self-actualizing steps are foregrounded:

> we make a burning territory
> Wherein there walk those influences of sky
> At that long moment of the eye
> When all leaps upward at some ancient wind
> Blown from the corners of some leaf-blocked road
> We walk upon in sober truth.
>
>   (N&SP, 167–68)

"Attempting to Persuade You to Go for a Walk in the Public Garden" (SFA, 74–75) may further illuminate these late poems, for the walk itself acts as a catalyst; the walker may walk uncon-scious desire into being. An invitation poem, civil and pleasure-oriented, in which the "simple and natural," lightness and ca-price, are evoked, the poem nevertheless dramatizes an awaken-ing in which movement is explicitly linked to desire:

It was the garden feeling,
It was the Eden good
Here by a lawn of water come
Upon it, to touch us,
Touch us, and let befall,
Stung into fire,
Helpless desire.

(SFA, 75)

Here desire is "helpless" because it cannot, ironically, be
"helped." Awakening creates disruption. Yet with disruption, as
Garrigue has suggested elsewhere, new knowledge and new
awareness of relationships between self and world may arise.

The possibility of making meaning becomes even more intricate for Garrigue as the late poem "Motifs from the Dark Wood"
(SFA, 78–80) makes clear. Memory is evoked—and as often occurs—is allied to water, here "water winding through rushes." As
images of the poem enter one another, morning and bird and
speaker and bird, the poem reflects Garrigue's change in approach; ellipses and ambiguous pronoun references create points
of silence, not so much evasions as markers of her increased
sense of a psychic accuracy composed of fragmentation.

Balladlike, the poem begins with an ambiguous abduction
scene that suggests the fused image of the loss of moonlike
consciousness, a lover, and the creative self:

My love was stolen from me,
Carried away like raw youth in a coach
Sang the dying voice of the morning
By a black shed where a bird was caught,
. . . .
Where the sanguineous carnation of the late-wintered sun
Reached out to lay its blood
On the blood of the bird,
The dusking webs inflamed by the rays,
Inflamed by the rays as by blood.

(SFA, 78)

A Persephone has been borne into the underworld. This central
figure must learn to speak of her own losses within the woodland's "most sinister conditions." Nevertheless, in this gothic
landscape she marks "this square of wood" (80), the page. Just as
Persephone metamorphoses into a queen within her underworld,

in Garrigue's late woodland the woman at the center of the wood
must transform herself.

As in "Studies for an Actress" the speaker attempts to be
inhabited, to be "spoken." And as in "Studies" the other who
would speak through the poem's persona "begins to and cannot."
The old webs of selfhood, like former "postures," must be "displayed" before she may speak:

> Who begins, who tries to speak
> As if through other lips
> Begins to and despairs,
> Begins to and cannot.
>
> (80)

Garrigue's metaphors suggest the enormity of the task. It is actually impossible "to speak through other lips." But here if we
assume that the power of the poetic mask is suggested, art actually may prove a saving struggle. Through her ability to contend,
the woman marks the page:

> Thereafter into the dark
> Who has eaten of the bird's heart.
> At every seventh step a drop of blood
> In the middle of this square of wood.
>
> (80)

The lyric poet who struggles for her art specifically eats "of the
bird's heart." She is pointedly a heroic figure—yet, we must note,
she is enclosed, pressed upon by a hostile environment.

Particularly illuminating in this context are women writers'
responses to space, specifically to enclosure, as they are explored
in Sandra Gilbert and Susan Gubar's The Madwoman in the
Attic. As Gilbert and Gubar have pointed out, women writers
may be aware that "'women's place' is itself irrational and
strange." As a consequence, women writers "translate into spa-
tial terms . . . despair at . . . spiritual constrictions." [10] More
recently, Deborah Pope has formulated the hypothesis that "the
imagery of enclosure, . . . as a consistent indicator of isolation,
recurs so frequently throughout women's writing that it can be
considered nearly archetypal."[11] Garrigue's exploration of con-
stricted space not only suggests her link to such a "nearly archetypal" pattern within women's writing but reflects her conscious
exploitation of the motif and her insistence on heroic gestures
within constricting circumstances. That her personae continu-

ously walk suggests their ability to mark the page and to attempt, despite constriction, to carve a space for themselves. Garrigue's emphasis on movement reflects her awareness of the importance of endurance. Judith Fryer in her study of the "spaces" that women writers occupy points out that in an attempt to create space for themselves, women writers seek to assume their own freedom. "Spaciousness . . . means being free; freedom implies space. It means having the power and enough room in which to act. It means having the ability to transcend the present condition, and that transcendence implies, quite simply, the power to move."[12] In this context, a portion of Garrigue's monograph on Marianne Moore may prove interesting. Garrigue wrote of Moore's symbolic city woodland:

> Two lines in "New York" might sound a theme: "one must stand outside and laugh / since to go in is to be lost." If these lines suggest that laughter can be a weapon of self-preservation, do they not also suggest a recognition of differences about which nothing can be done? It is essential not to go in and be lost. (MM, 10–11)

Apparently, however, Garrigue's initial estimate caused her some ambivalence. Nineteen pages later she returns to Moore's poem and suggests another reading. Referring to Moore's appropriation of Henry James's phrase "accessibility to experience," she notes, "*Accessibility* suggests that one may go inside, even be lost, agreeably." She enters her woodland as a means of making accessible diffuse psychic forces and to contend with them through her own efforts at dynamism. Self-consciously, she erects her motif as a means of presenting conflict.

The following poem—the final poem of *Studies for an Actress*—culminates with this poet's allegiance to shape shifting and desire as her sources of authority. Again we are within a woodland, and pointedly the opening of "Moondial" visually echoes that of "The Flux of Autumn." And yet this is less "golden burst" than burned field:

> To speak of this hot day: the flaming fields
> Filled to the brim with scorch, tasting of singe
> And bake and brown: those gasping trees, some dying
> At the top: a tangle of long-legged flowers,
> Their faces put askew upon their stalks,
> And Queen Anne's lace as slant on crooked stems. . . .
>
> (SFA, 81)

A present seared by a lifetime of intense experience may be
redeemed through the authority of imagination and desire. Garrigue's progression toward burning is prefigured in "This Day Is
Not Like That Day" in which the "rapt mind [is] burning long / In
its visions, which vanished" (MR, 12). Experience had been, as in
one of her earliest poems, cruciblelike: "I saw how easily we
start— / Our hearts in us that so desire the fire" (E&C, 65). Most
significantly, a gathering of moonlight as imagination's "stuff"
serves her as a reference for the self's own capacity to illuminate.

> We walked in moonstuff, lawn and tissue of it,
> Past forests chained by it and molded so
> That levels of its fountains of dark growth,
> Tier upon tier of rich, broad-plated leaves,
> Were sculptured by the massy flood,
> Fey governor of the insubstantial.
>
> (SFA, 82)

Forests, so often places of claustrophobia and limitation in the
poet's earlier work, are sculpted by moonlight and as such rendered benificent and artfully shaped through female power. The
moon emerges as a second creative self, similar to the "all-
mothering stuff" of "The Flux of Autumn." And as in "The Flux
of Autumn" and "Motifs from the Dark Wood," the woman
makes, through a bodily poetics of movement, the outward design of her desires. The speaker and a companion "walked . . . by
the harvests of the moonlight": and from a forest passed into
"pastures where it browsed, / Our blameless phantom." "We
walked in moonstuff"; "And walked we by the harvest of the
light"; "And walked by over-arching boughs, down grass-rimmed
roads . . ." (82). This poet creates a form of water walk, for her
poem is organized around the action of walking and the images
of moonlight and landscape described in terms of fluids, further
reinforcing her emphasis on shape-changing consciousness. The
road is "splashed by shade," and the lane erupts with "fountains
of dark growth," a "massy flood," the "foam" and "spray" of
moonlight that the walkers "dip . . . [their] hands in . . . to the
wrists" (82). The inspiration of the moon is fluid: "We drank the
air that drank of moon, / Deceptions that it practiced . . ." (84).
Creative illusion is both a restorative and a philter. As with her
fountains, illusion and movement, especially vertical movement,
dominate the poem. The forest is mazelike, its limits blurred and
dissolved in favor of a psychic alchemy in which this poet

reveals the actively receptive and female-aligned moonlight as a valid and clarifying vision: "Each semi-tropic, half Italianate leaf / Seemed so defined you'd think a draughtsman's pen / Had cut it out of air" (82). A new precision is effected. And here are the imagistic elements—muse as moonlight, webs as self-display, woodlands, and water walks—that she has focused upon for thirty years, transformed.

She concludes by praising metamorphosis and moonlike consciousness that, as in "Studies for an Actress," creates a "binding element," significantly a female element, that makes the poem possible:

> I raise again these moon-splashed fields,
> Like half-remembered legends I recount
> How apparitions skeined us in a coil
> Where wholly given, wholly found,
> Our beings' threads were wound,
> Secessions, then, by sun!
> But not from the One.
>
> (SFA, 85)

Through a "reversed step" from the blighted present to a redeemed past, Garrigue renders moonlight as not only a "supernatural substance" but a queenly figure similar to her actress. Rather than hoarding her power or ensnaring others, the moon empowers others by "shedding" weblike rays; she does not lose power but through her generosity displays it and inspires those who have the necessary faculties to appeal to her.

In "Moondial" Garrigue then draws together her motifs. She identifies with a source of light, the moon as shape-changing symbol of strange flux. The woman of the poem enters into a ritualistic relationship to her environment in ways similar to the rites presided over by Garrigue's performers. Her speaker's affections are similarly enlarged. Through the walk Garrigue focuses upon a landscape seemingly volatized and a figure who may physically and spiritually enter into new relationships with her surroundings.

As early as 1944, in the introduction to her first collection of poems, the poet's objective to both preserve the moment and follow the fact of change were fully conscious:

> The forestation of symbol around all of the events that have the integrity which obliges the poet to use them, the funereal fact which in the jostle and evaporation of all which, as soon as it happens, is

changing, the quartz sides, the lengthening perspectives of objects, these are all a part of that memoranda so impressive and moving. . . . If [the poet] "saves" it is also because he saves what he has changed. He changes what he sees, redefines and establishes new analogues, disparities, cousinships, . . . (*TSP*, 86)

In water walks Garrigue found movement that mirrors the process of assuming a desirous imaginative identity. The walker may herself embody the power of ambitious transformation. While water for Garrigue is a resource that the poem simultaneously may describe and emulate, by writing of a persona in movement, she makes seeking more generously contemplative than willfully aggrandizing. She places herself "at the sweet borders of chance." If as in "The Dominant House" we are to believe that "the truth is in the scene of sensation" (*N&SP*, 136), Garrigue composes mutable scenes to assume a truth of flux.

POSTSCRIPT

Among her later poems Garrigue wrote a kind of epitaph, "Doggerel of a Diehard Who Sleeps in a Nest of Newspapers."[1] The poem, uncollected, is striking, for it records Garrigue's sense that she labored to "fill rooms with light":

> Boughs I brought into my room
> Cut from the trunk.
> They flower that won't have fruit
> Who fill my room with light.
> No epitaph for that.

Garrigue's diehard is indeed dying hard, as the self-mocking title suggests. In a metaphorics dependent on some suggestion of natural rather than commodified beauty, Garrigue mourns what she perceives as cultural repudiation of feeling and beauty. The poem revolves from the playful to the cynical, from the colloquial to the highly burnished. "[T]hose neat engines that convert / The Real into The Ideal!" have failed everyone, it would seem. The parting lines of the poem suggest Garrigue's acknowledgment that she labored "cut from" her "source"—whether from a respected women's tradition or from a societal awareness of beauty that goes beyond objective "use":

> Who would praise the flowering bough
> That had no purpose for its flower
> And, cut from its source,
> Flowered anyhow?

"The flower that won't have fruit" is a flower that evades us, that will not declare a product to be used. The revealing pronoun "who" personifies the flower and suggests Garrigue's own resistance. Although not nurtured, cut from a source, the flower fills a room with light. There is "no epitaph for that" precisely because no epitaph is quite to the point. The flowers that "fill" a room "with light" provide their own radiant answer as Garrigue challenges the reader to adjust expectations to her own renewing "tradition": as a woman and as a poet she may indeed be the cut branch, forming, even under negligent external conditions, the multiples of flower and light. "Strewn over, the very eye strewn / With the light of the flower and the hum of light," Garrigue makes a pact to see complexly, to see "even, at the base of the tree, / A few [flowers] sprouting there. . . ."[2] She means to see at least doubly, to see not one object of sight alone but the "object's" relationship to more than one.

"If there is any truth it is in the relationship," Garrigue wrote in the introduction to her first collection of poems. To bring a particular "into its warmest world" (*TSP*, 84) became her quest. The flowers that she would write of throughout her career— vervain, Queen Anne's lace, veronica, bloodroot, crocuses, harebells, oleander, chrysanthemums, and most essentially the rose—are imaged as fleeting forms of light that nevertheless belie their seeming fragility by withstanding nature's extremes and cyclically renewing. Self-renewal through the transformative power of the imagination informs her poems. Through returning to central images she deepens her awareness of transformation. As such, Garrigue resembles the gardener of *Country Without Maps* who asks that growth come to her as well as to the garden she works: "Let me have your wild surprise / Yes, and tell me on my knees / Of your new life" (57).

APPENDIX

The Grand Canyon

Where is the restaurant cat?
I am lonely under the fluorescent light
as a cook waddles in her smoky region visible through an open
    arch
and someone is pounding, pounding
whatever it is that is being pounded
and a waitress cracks with the cowboys lined up at the counter
lumberjacked, weathered and bony
intimates, I would guess, of the Canyon,
like the raven that flies, scouting above it,
of the hooked face and the almost flat sleek wings.

Where is my cat? I am lonely,
knocked out, stunned-sleepy,
knocked out by the terraced massed faces
of the brute Sublime,
color inflamed,
when I came to the edge and looked over:
violaceous, vermillion
great frontal reefs, buttes,
cliffs of rufous and ocher angles,
promontories, projections, jutments, outjuttings
and gnarled mirlitons, so it seemed,
twisting up out of depth beyond depth
gnarled like the juniper tree
rachitic with wind I hung on to
as the raven's wing, glassy in the light of its black,
slid over me

there at the edge of this maw, gash
deepest in the world that a river has made
through an upwarp in the earth's crust,
thickets of tens of thousands of gorges eaten out

by freezing and thawing, tempests, waterspouts,
squalls and falls of the river
with its boulders, pebbles, silt and sand sawing down
through the great cake of geologic time,
eight layers laid bare,
the total effect creating what geometrical effect
in a rocky silence so clear
a bird's voice, even a boy's
is spunged out, sucked up by this stillness
stinging, overpowering the ear,
pure condition of the original echoing soundlessness
this voluminous wrung resonance
welling up out of the handiwork
of the demiurge wrestling down there
in an infinity of imperceptible events
some ten million years,

ages blanching to think of,
taking the switchback trail,
slipping and sliding,
forever slantwise descending
into new confrontations of parapets,
chimneys, mantels, segments of angles,
modelings of rock of slacknesses and accidental tensions
combined with the effects of its weight—
the total effect never total for never can you see it all, not even
     guess
at mazes of the proliferation,
and the river will not be visible
except from a driven angle,
the snaken twists of its rapids looking petrified, frozen
from the distance of a deep mile:

somebody saying a mountain could be plucked up by its roots
and dropped head-first down there and it wouldn't dam up the
     river
so that the waters would run over

and that the Washington Monument could be kept out of the
     rain
under one overhanging of an otherwise vertical red wall
where the gold of the light on that chaos of creases nervously
     darts

like the violet-green swallow stitching its leaps and arcs
over the gliding raven,

over the camber of columns, tawny rotundas of ruins
writhed, mottled, crested with shells,
escarpments
downbeaten by frost and rain,
parallel rangings of
rostrums, pulpits and lecterns,
and the mad Tiberius arches groining
cave holes on cave holes in the same wall of limestone, red
from the ironstone drippings,

Aztec pyramidal temples rising in hundreds of steps
to the summit of the seemed shrine
curtained, girdled with snakes and necklaces of hearts,
wet with sacrificial blood,

rusticated building blocks jutting out in warlike ramifications of
    forts,
stockades of black frosted rock,
towers of the baldness mounting like obelisks,
pyramidal forms from the sands of Egypt,
crags vertiginous, cupolas, alcoves,
amphitheatres, arenas, organ pipes, flutings,
porches of rock, wedges of shadow in perforated rock,

and the gold of the light nervously darting
on the Bright Angel shale, pink with long stripes,
on the lavender blue of the Shinumo Quartzite,
on the deeper rose of the Hakatai shale,
on the blond Coconino sandstone
riddled, it's said, with the trails of sea worms,
on the grey Kaibab limestone
with casts of shark teeth and horn coral imbedded
like the Hermit shale of the topmost formation
with footprints of salamanders, insect wings four inches in
    length
and even a dimple left by a raindrop during some era of burning
and hailstorm, torrent and drought,
era on era stacked here,
untold era on era,

as the eye like a long-legged insect on a windowpane
slithers and shudders up and down
the banded and ribboned, ribbed systems of rock,
into and out of shadows,
chromatic world of what glitters like phantoms,
corrugations of scaffoldings appointing to chill
over the continuous surface,
assemblies of aggregations
sand-pocked and pitted,
ridged, wind-serrated,
tawny threshholds in the lying out there of the steeps,
in the drinking up of the stillness
pressed in by the gorged rock
deepening in the light of the motes of beams
under those clouds that like water lilies
enclose within them this silence received
that they graze upon and are gone.

(*Studies for an Actress and Other Poems*, pp. 68–71)

Studies for an Actress
(After having heard Galina Vishnevskaya sing in Dubrovnik)

What she has known, how may our hearts surmise?
Grace that is willful, wit that alerts
Misfortune that it jests with to attract
That she disarms then by a daring step,
Her heart grown richer by this peril met.
And yet a circumstance too small and tight
And she, estranged, cannot invent.
A cloudy counterfeiting takes her up,
Imbroglio of play to which she's card,
The trump they slap, the queen of restless mouth
In that quick living crowding towards the grave.

Yet turn on her the hour she's long rehearsed,
Some knife-edge of the pillaged and profaned,
She pivots on her heel and she is Faith
Like one who stands upon a balcony
Above strange ruins in rooms and streets below
That hordes new loosed like rumors from their masks
Now run upon, more dark than dream,

The which she meets with such a scorn of calm
You'd think she knew a triumph that could come
From something more than malice and than wrong
And this outfacing brings her prisoners—
Lovers who'd have their eyes put out
By such a gathered radiance.

One instant then, and she has veered
When those light things called thoughts
Solidify, grow obdurate as rock.
She flees all action now, she has gone in
Upon a demi-day that sinks towards night
Under instruction from the strangest powers
She would appease and cannot, who reveal
In the most obscure and sinking down of ways
This that they want which will fulfill
This that she does not know, which she must do.
Can she turn back? The path is overgrown.
Ahead,
Roads like lines in the palms of the dead
Now fade.

And must she be who cannot be
This that she scarcely knows she lives
Which baffles in its large, impersonal strength
(Beyond herself and borrowed from the race)
Except that she has guessed it deviously
And it takes over now and glitters out. . . .
We saw her coming, tilted on her heels
Pale her mouth, her body cast aside,
Quick knowledge made it light as any shroud

And eagerness, the rashness of a child,
Envisaging such pleasures as
Riding in a carriage in a fall of flowers
Contracted to that fine formality
That comes upon the soul when it perceives
Just what deceiving passions must take leave.

Is it a play of cross-grained theme
That she would have it that she's acting in
In an unbelievable, intemperate zone
Aloft with figures dwelling in the skies

Big-backed, with arms upraised, in stony robes,
Saluting reverberations in the clouds
Or then—the muted, trembling time
When ailing of her differences or not
She is no more than mere
Dissembling in a mirror?

Soggietto mitologico of this known theme?
Denote her history, if you will, by scenes
If that is how a life can be summed up
Except she believes her differing masks hide no one
But what the action brought to her to be
As if they were a foreign element
That she put on and then put off,
Performing in them alien acts,
The I that was another, that odd she.

And so she thought until the prince of shades
Got into the broad bed where she lay propped.
This was a nuptial scene beyond all doubt
For he would extract from her sleep-bound head
By dense green shadows laced there by a tree
The moon, the stars that grow on boughs,
The moon in her horn drawn by a griffin,
Everything eyed and starred,
Feet bounding like swallows tilting off earth,
The bounding feet of mirth

And then those figures fixed upon a point
Forever at their height and in their hour
When flushed they pierce the dragon's jaw
Or bring the severed head back home,
Who do not change thereafter, tire, nor want
For they are of the fixéd state
Of emblematic figures outside time—
That armored angel on his horse reared back
In wild-eyed excitement—

These crowd the habitations of her sleep
And are not kindly when she wakes,
Garbed figures, rapt and wrought
All to one aim and ending, blazonries
Like constellations of a zodiac

She pulls against and yet is driven by,
And she would ask these players of the immense
Pardon for her fitfulness.

And yet to all this she has come very late
And she forgets, she loses then her place.
We see them at the height of their excess
Who do not change thereafter, tire, nor want
And she is of the shuttling flux
That knows extinction even as it's born,
And she is sightless now with flagging search
That cannot state its end.

A leaf that falls upon a book,
An autumn of a young day come too soon,
And she has lost the thread that let
Those emblems forth, that rich connecting
Between their powers and broad awaking.
Deep knowledge dressed their concentrates.
Then had she moved in such a light of it
As if beneath their very protectorate.
Now, dying bell notes decrescendoing!

And so she falls half out of life,
Out of the net of things into the dark,
Who has no strength now for that bright-in-dark,
That second life those emblemed figures knit.
Blind fit. Nothing to hold her back from this descent
Into a void, opaque, unlit,
When out from feeling, cut the links,
Like torches quenched in sand.
And this is a kind of falling-out she also knows
A kind of hero flails. Which she cannot.
Caught now in her alternatings
Before the incessant intervenings, changings,
And this is twice-known, many-times-more-known
Indifferent death, suggestible on every hand
To light and just as soon converted to the dark.

II

There is a binding element
The which when had, sustains the crazy shifts

Of mind, the turnings and the twistings of the heart,
And those odd twins, the wish and will,
And which, when known, assembles, gathers up
All that will sustain and nourish it.
And is it this that forged the angel's smile,
The gay stone lips, the strong wings folded back,
And is it this of which the poplars speak
Glittering and shouting in the full, strong morning light
And is it this in gaunt cathedrals raised
Of shadows steeped on shadows, mountainous space?

And is it of the mind or heart?
Half human, is it more than that?
And can you give it names like joy, desire,
Like expectation, hope, or triumph known?
Is it of essence alien to the name,
Alien to time, beyond the body's will?
You seek for it, it cannot be invoked. . . .

But if it's lost, the key is lost,
The light is out, all is inert and stony,
What's loved it is not known one loves
Nor is the bird beheld, its stripes denoted,
Its savage black head with the open bill,
Its rosy-russet wings half spread
In battle with another bird
Over a helpless beetle, taken to heart
Nor taken to heart the *festoni* on the *ara*,
The godded bull's horns rising out of ivy,
The true and single government
Of the anthology of forms.

It is of the airiness of apparition
And what has not been founded on a legend?
Great cities had their start in such a light
As when after a battle someone saw
The famous horsemen, half-god brothers,
The famous offspring of the swan-loved Leda,
(The round-eyed ones according to a sculptor)
Watering their horses at a spring.
Until they came there was no spring,
They struck it forth the way they came from air,

Sign there in the Forum on which all turned
To prophesy how Fortune would grow great.

And this she knows and does not know
Assailed by knowledge of a plenitude
The dense, packed world refutes in paining ways.
The world is real, so was the spring that gushed,
So are the rough-cut stones that house what would deny
All that we see. The world is real, and are her falterings real,
And is her weakness truth, her vacillations?
That wending in between the gulfs,
That effort to create the links,
The correspondences how difficult, unfixed,
To set and fix?

And what but the mind sustains the cross-gained theme?
She judges this in that immoderate light
In which the monuments are set.
As to the stones and pillars it gives voice,
Those involutions, that crazed checkerwork
That if it or heart not open out,
Stand in their splendor mute.

She prays now to the smallest thing
Under the black brocade of pines,
She prays for the wind muffled in them,
For the fields in the shimmer of butterflies,
For valerian, dianthus, columbine,
She prays to pray, but cannot start.

Now to the violet light she recommends
When skies open into skies
That clamor of the throng of voices
Kept down, locked in, but murmurous as bees
Ready as ever for the nuptial flight,
Passionate, wholly passionate.

She prays if nothing else to be
In some dissolving medium of light,
A pond that's set to catch the arrowy beams,
Reflective and obedient as that.
She prays then to change

If it's in changing that things find repose.
She prays to praise. She prays to be
Condensed now to one desire
As if it were very life performing her.

(*Studies for an Actress and Other Poems*, pp. 2–8)

After Reading
The Country of the Pointed Firs

She was the one who lived up country
Half in the woods on a rain-washed road
With a well not near and a barn too far
And the fields ledgy and full of stones
That the crows cawed over and liked to walk in
And the hills and the hollow thick with fern
And in the swamp the cattails and rushes.

It was next to living in a town of birds
But she had hens and a row of bee hives.
When her mother died, and her girl, and Joel,
She told the bees so they'd not fly away
And hung black flags on the doors of the hives
Though they'd always go when they could to the woods
Or swarm on Sunday when she was at meeting.
For each who went she had told the bees.

Change and loss was what the brook cried
That she heard in the night—but she kept snug
With crow-wood for kindling, and the sun shone good
Through the tops of the pines, and her plants
Didn't fail her, and the rosebush always bloomed
By the gnawed fencepost—what the horse had done
When they had a horse and a cow and a dog.

O there had been many, and now was there none?
Lost at sea, they said, her son gone to sea
Lost at sea they said. But if he wasn't
And if he'd come back—so she'd stay till he came
Or whether or not.
Change and loss was what the brook cried
That she heard in the night when the clock whirred.

But when the fog from the southbank came through the firs
Till the air was like something made of cobwebs,
Thin as a cobweb, helpless as shadows
Swept here and there as the sea gulls mewed,
O then it seemed it was all one day
And no one gone and no one crossed over
Or when the rain gurgled in the eave spout
Or the wind walked on the roof like a boy.

Change and loss was what the brook cried
That she heard in the night when the clock whirred
Just before it clanged out its twelve heavy strokes
In the thick of the stillness, black as a crow,
But no scritching now with a scrawny great crackling,
And the rain not trickling, nothing to hark to,
Not even the tree at the north chamber window.

Till she routed it, horse and foot,
Thinking of walking to town through pastures
When the wood thrushes wept their notes
And the moss was thick on the cobbled stones
With the heron wading among the hummocks
Of the pursy meadow that went down to the sea.

And she had knitting and folks to visit,
Preserves to make, and cream tartar biscuit,
She knew where was elocamp, coltsfoot, lobelia,
And she'd make a good mess up for all as could use it,
And go to the well and let down the bucket
And see the sky there and herself in it
As the wind threw itself about in the bushes and shouted
And another day fresh as a cedar started.

(*Studies for an Actress and Other Poems*, pp. 19–20)

For the Fountains and Fountaineers of Villa d'Este

Say that these are the fireworks of water,
One hundred fountains on the tiers of plains;
That goddesses enthroned hold spears of it,
It erupts from the mouths of shagged eagles,
And moss-legged gods, one side of the face worn off by it,

Straddle the silver, unmitigated flood.
Say that the down play and up play
And fourteen shafts around a central plume
Not to discount the dragons spouting it
That meet two dolphins plunged in it
Sending their streams against the contending ones,
Are a continuum in a series of play by water
And play by light on the water, making arcs
Of a spectrum in the din and bafflement
Of that most muffled watery bell beat, pell mell and lulled
    stampede,
So that an insatiable thirst
Cannot be allayed in the blood.
Though they flow round the very bones,
Though a tumult of vapor rising from them
Blows the leaves of the tree by their weight,
Nothing, no, not by any rain-making vows.
Nor any meandering of boughs
Down the stone-flagged paths and the avenues
Of the serpentine oleander
Whose branch knots and slippering leaves
Knit such a shade in the place of green light
It is a scandal of pleasure,
Say that nothing, no limestone grotto alive
With the sibylline god gushing forth
This silver, non-potable liquid,
Can convey to the fever coolness
Nor a slaking, a quenching by dews
Where the scent of the water buds.

Here are fans of water, and silver combs,
Peacock-eyed in the sun-glints upon them,
Vines and wreaths trailed round a stone,
And thirst has become a delirium,
It heaps on the brain,
It plunges along the arm,
In a sleep by leaves
It buries half the blood.
Taking one sinuous course down the breast
It would thrust and lock round the heart in a trice.

While, to stand, sheathed in a grotto
On the reverse side of this shield of water,

Downpouring in pound on pound
Its chafed, silver-shot metal . . .
I know of no fury that tells
More to me, deafening, than that
Of a velocity past which I'd know
Nothing but the hurl and fall
Of those burst rockets of water
Driving their sweetness into the ground
In a blaze of lightnings and stars
As in wet dusts shattering on stone
To explode with soft fury again.

Shield of the water and water wall,
Water roots, tentacles, bars,
Spears of water and bolts,
I know nothing here but the sense
In this downflowing fall
Of the wilderness of eternity.
And I am flailed to earth.
I am dank as a river god.
Scallop on scallop of the primeval flat water leaf
With no roots but in water, taking its substance from liquid,
Coats me and jackets me over.
I am dense as lichen,
Primordial as fern,
Or, like that tree split at its base,
Covert for winter creatures and water-retreated life,
Tip with my boughs very serpent green,
Or in a grand spirit of play
Spurt water out of my nostrils.

Veins and gaddings of water,
I have seen you in a fall
Shoot madness into a marble,
And ever the thud and *pronk* of the pump,
Hee-haw and frog *harrumph!*, that heave and rail
Of the mechanical works
That create the genius of water flowing . . .

To tread the crests of the fountains,
To walk on the foam of their flowers,
Upthrust in a vertical climbing
Spires of the falling and changing stuff

In a ghost play of dance
Creating beyond their climbing
Caps of their vapor, a white turbulence
Of that which so changes beyond them
It is sur-foam, surf-combed,
It is got by the mathematics of climbing—
To reach by those aerobatics into white snows of the
    mounting—
There to dissolve into
What brings all the condensed fury of dews
Back down into descending.

To dance on those heavy heads of water
So richly and artfully sustained
By white prongs and tongues of the air
Curdling up liquid from nowhere,
The advance and the sword of a watery swirl
That is somehow compact with air,
Or to take from the lull
Of the deep music such a dream
As will not abandon flame,
To sink into the deep-blown
Horn-called music and the wind-
Flung and cheek-puffed
Surge and hee-ho-hum of the thing . . .
Shagged eagles that do not spout
By *fleur de lys*, all moss, that do,
And the shafts then and the boat-shaped urn—
Three kinds of shapes of water flowing
Across two kinds of spouts descending
And one out of the mouths of horned or big-eared animal gods.

A water walk by all this bewildering
Fantasy of arising and falling flutes of the water,
Columned water adorned, making a gush and warble of sound.

    II
Fountains, if to behold you
Were to have rain down over me
The least tendril and slightest shoot
Of your very white jubilation!
In the coil of your spirits be wound!
Or wrapped in your sleek skins

Mortality itself unfitted,
Made wild as it was, bound in rings
Of the lightly springing-up streams
That go in a series of crystal hoops
And twenty such hoops you have,
Twenty wickets of running light
In glittering slivers of it
Set in an *Alice* water garden
Where the cultivation is water, not earth,
Stamens and stems of water stuff,
Emblems of water pouring from emblems,
Griffons that jut it, like merry she-gods
Winged at the back but firm fish-tailed
From whose breasts spurt the magnificent jets!

As I beheld you down levels of grass,
Throwing out the wild mists of forgetfulness.
Gashing down through the tender grace
Of a green confinement by slopes.
White channels were a most beautiful thing,
Channels, chalk white, with the sluice's spume
Were a most beautiful, astonishing thing
Coursing with mad dog race down the grass
From one fountainous place to the next.
As I saw you in bird-frail seines
Down a green depth of height.
Sinews and locks fine as veils
Showing all vegetation behind them,
Chains, flashing and weaving,
Strands as of links of snow
Released and transformed into air.
Below, a deep chasm, a tangled abyss
Only a bird may sift, flying down the crevasse
For a sip from a luminous beam.

(Are there not butterflies for these surf-flowers?
Do not tell me that one ever drowned.
Lingering too long by the gust of some fountain,
Or that those twinkling in teams, parting and closing
The light-dotted vanes of their wings
Ever capsized, riding over a stream
The way song soaring rides down a wind.)

Fountains, our volatile kin,
Coursing as courses the blood,
For we are more water than earth
And less of flesh than a flame
Bedded in air and run by the wind—
Bequeath me, be with me, endow my hunger
With sweet animal nature,
Knit me in with the plumes and the wands of your favor,
Get me great vistas, jade-milky streams
Where the source of the fury starts,
Winking up the last supper of light.
Get me chrysanthemums, great bulky heads,
And a stem narrow as mercury
Fit to support a bluet.
And out of the reflections of water on stone
Let me count the great arcs,
The clusters rounded as grapes
Or staccato as needles,
All that momentum kept firm
Propelled by the dry force of form—
To rest, momentarily at least
In the cataract of time—
Leaves for his feathers on the breast of an eagle,
Deep light of the long nights and years!

        III
In this tranquil life such as belongs to windmills
Though the subtle day does not blow
But stands tranced in the wickets
And aspirations of water,
Descend by these paths, these perspectives,
This cascade of steps by the balustrades
Downgliding as if molded out of waves,
Into the white strata and springs
Of the founding place and wedding of waters.
But you must thrice interpret to know.
Mad on the waters, what they vow. . . .
Listen. The fine battery of them.
Like a purification of sound
Blows their deep chanting,
That murmurous persisting.
No wilier song from the moon

Ever plunged into and took apart,
Dividing the plangent strands of it,
Such a fine cornucopia of bloom.

Like a low meditation on song
Before that song has begun,
This speech over you in a mesh,
This chain-mail of running light and of breath,
This tissue as if of sleep
That is so lightly woven
The dream stares through with its Bacchic locks
Till you wear the very cloth of dream at last
Of figured and intertwined emblems.
Walks in long arches under it,
Portals through which if you go
You are into the white-woven web held fast.
But you must thrice interpret to tell
What is said by a flower in a spell,
Ascending the steps to the gods . . .
You may see them among the flowers,
Standing small-headed, vast-eyed,
The grace of the broad breast turned,
A beardful of weeds and small ones
Lurked there by the marble-veined sides.

And you have gone the ways of each sense
To dam up thirst or to stanch it.
There was a wild stream lashed to a tree
Gave out its oracular oratory.
By a flume came thrasonical volley
Boasting of love and struggle.
Through watery walls blown asunder,
So light the small threads of structure,
By so many gadding ways of the senses
Harnessed to water, knowing what fire
Must make their divine toil turn wheels
For the relentless mills and wills
You came from the watery furnaces,
From springs sealed of the sleep
Smoldering with what divinations
If such may arise and wake.

And meanwhile they stand there, they linger,
They recline, they preside, in languor or rigors,
Gods, our great friends of love and rage.
Passion stares into their empty eyes
Want sees the calm sweet water coursing,
Artfully held in their mouths and pulsing,
Blind waters tranquilly stemming there.

(New and Selected Poems, pp. 64–72)

Motifs from the Dark Wood

I

My love was stolen from me,
Carried away like raw youth in a coach
Sang the dying voice of the morning
By a black shed where a bird was caught,
Fluttering and clawing, its eye
Liquid with the glycerine of crying,
Its low warble as it strove webbed-over,
Caught in the threads of that stooped porthole
That gave on the east, sea of cloud,
Where the sanguineous carnation of the late-wintered sun
Reached out to lay its blood
On the blood of the bird,
The dusking webs inflamed by the rays,
Inflamed by the rays as by blood.

Like our childhood troubled in the lost park
At the coming of night on a low-clouded evening
And the slowing down of the rhythms
In the paling of light and the quieting
As the edge of the wood thickens
Into which the vespers of small green voices
Have huskily entered and halted . . .
Coming from meadows at sunset
Seen through the tarlatan of blossom
How slow our walking, our pausing,
Dawdling over the bridges

By water winding through rushes.
Outbursts of voices! A sudden star!

Can we ever not linger, delay . . .
On a pond of moon that lolling sail
May flare us out on a far journey . . .
Rifflings and ebbings, departures . . .
Your hand on mine unsettling me
As music would a tree.

II

The brambled chase in the rides of the forest
As the wind blew its hunting horn.
Following after its notes under leaves,
Through the down-reaching boughs of fir,
Parting our way through them and briar,
Till we came to the twilit avenue
Of trees in ill-set rows
By a brook engorged, gone green and broad,
And the passage of whispers done.

Was it here we dreamed we saw
In a round-centered point like a grove
A spreading-antlered stag and doe
Beside a shaft of stone fenced round
By sparse, rigid iron
And further palisading it
Rivals as of unknown flowers
Blanche-tall but crimson-mouthed.

It was like a chapeled grove
So wan the light come down.
Set deep in moss the name
On this neglected thing.
Abruptions of a light
When an eddying wind might bring
A kind of shudder back . . .

And what begins again,
What begins, who tries to speak
As if through webs upon the mouth,

Who begins, who tries to speak
As if through other lips
Begins to and despairs,
Begins to and cannot.

Moth! What has happened!
You that appear!
O in the wood wept
Drawn on by that fey . . .

Thereafter into the dark
Who has eaten of the bird's heart.
At every seventh step a drop of blood
In the middle of this square of wood.

(*Studies for an Actress and Other Poems*, pp. 78–80)

NOTES

Introduction

1. Theodore Roethke, "Five American Poets," *New World Writing* (New York: New American Library, 1953), 85.

2. Harvey Shapiro, "The Journey through a Poem," *New York Times* 22 June (1973): 33.

3. Robert Lowell, publisher's blurb, *Country Without Maps* (New York: Macmillan, 1964).

4. Adrienne Rich, review of *Studies for an Actress and Other Poems*, *American Poetry Review* September–October (1973): 43.

5. Stephen Stepanchev, "Jean Garrigue," *American Poetry Since 1945: A Critical Survey* (New York: Harper, 1965), 92.

6. Babette Deutsch, *Poetry in Our Time* (New York: Columbia University Press, 1956), 94–95.

7. Laurence Lieberman, "The Body of the Dream," *Unassigned Frequencies: American Poetry in Review, 1964–77* (Urbana: University of Illinois Press, 1977), 108.

8. Stanley Kunitz, "Jean Garrigue (1913–72): A Symposium," ed. Mary Anne Shea, *Twentieth-Century Literature* 29 (1983):13.

9. Jean Garrigue in "Jean Garrigue," *Contemporary Authors*, ed. Barbara Harte and Carolyn Riley (Detroit: Gale, 1969), 423.

10. Jean Garrigue, in Jean Gould, "Jean Garrigue," *Modern American Women Poets* (New York: Dodd, 1984), 98.

11. Jean Garrigue in *Twentieth-Century Authors*, ed. Stanley Kunitz and Howard Haycraft (New York: H. W. Wilson, 1955), 354.

12. Marjorie Garrigue Smith, "Jean Garrigue (1913–72): A Symposium," 4.

13. In *Twentieth-Century Authors*, 354.

14. Ibid.

15. Randall Jarrell, "Poetry in War and Peace," *Partisan Review* 12 (1945): 123.

16. John Berryman, review of *The Ego and the Centaur*, *Partisan Review* 15 (1948): 261.

17. Louise Bernikow, introduction, *The World Split Open: Four Centuries of Women Poets in England and America, 1552–1950* (New York: Random House, 1974) 3.

18. Stanley Kunitz, "Jean Garrigue," *A Kind of Order, a Kind of Folly: Essays and Conversations* (Boston: Little, Brown 1975), 256.

19. John Frederick Nims, "The Poetry of Sylvia Plath," *Ariel Ascending: Writings About Sylvia Plath*, ed. Paul Alexander (New York: Harper, 1985), 49.

20. Cheryl Walker, *The Nightingale's Burden: Women Poets and Culture Before 1900* (Bloomington: Indiana University Press, 1982), 143.

21. Luce Irigaray, *This Sex Which Is Not One*, trans. Catherine Porter with Carolyn Burke (Ithaca: Cornell University Press, 1985), 30–31.

22. Estella Lauter, *Women as Mythmakers: Poetry and Visual Art by Twentieth-Century Women* (Bloomington: Indiana University Press, 1984), 212.

23. Nina Auerbach, *Woman and the Demon: The Life of a Victorian Myth* (Cambridge: Harvard University Press, 1982), 228.

1. "The Excessive Language of Light": Jean Garrigue's "Restless Eye"

1. See John Berger's *About Looking* (New York: Pantheon, 1980). I am indebted to Berger, who stresses that seeing is never a neutral activity but must involve choice.

2. Laurence Lieberman, "Jean Garrigue: The Body of the Dream," 115.

3. Anne Hollander, "Moving Pictures," *Raritan* 5, no. 3 (1986): 89.

4. Jean Garrigue in *Contemporary Poets of the English Language*, ed. Rosalie Murphy (Chicago: St. James, 1970), 405.

5. Jean Garrigue, "The Angel of the Graveyard," *International Literary Annual*, ed. John Wain (London: John Calder, 1959) 101–2.

6. Jean Garrigue in *Twentieth-Century Authors*, 355.

7. Hyatt H. Waggoner, *American Visionary Poetry* (Baton Rouge: Louisiana State University Press, 1982), 10.

8. John Berger, "Why Look at Animals?" in *About Looking*, 11.

9. Ibid., 19

10. Ibid., 21.

11. Babette Deutsch, *Poetry in Our Time*, 95.

12. Jean Garrigue's letter to Louise Bogan is quoted in Elizabeth Frank's *Louise Bogan: A Portrait* (New York: Knopf, 1985), 322.

13. Howard Nemerov, review of *The Monument Rose*, *Sewanee Review* 62 (1954) 317.

2. Each an "Odd She": Strange Performers

1. Jean Garrigue, in *Twentieth-Century Authors*, 355.

2. Mary K. DeShazer, *Inspiring Women: Reimagining the Muse* (New York: Pergamon, 1986), 2.

3. Ibid., 3.

4. Babette Deutsch, *Poetry Handbook: A Dictionary of Terms* (New York: Funk, 1974) 19.

5. Jane Mayhall, "The Values of the Tentative," *New Leader* 29 January 1968: 23.

6. Sarah Orne Jewett, "The Country of the Pointed Firs," *The Country of the Pointed Firs and Other Stories*, ed. Mary Ellen Chase (New York: Norton, 1968), 49.

7. Laurence Lieberman, "Jean Garrigue: The Body of the Dream," 110.

8. Helen Vendler, *Part of Nature, Part of Us: Modern American Poets* (Cambridge: Harvard University Press, 1980), 305.

9. Laurence Lieberman, "Jean Garrigue: The Body of the Dream," 110–11.

3. Threatening Romance: The Subversive Heart

1. Stephen Stepanchev, "Jean Garrigue," *American Poetry Since 1945: A Critical Survey*, 87.

2. "Boy's Resume at Twenty-Three," *College Verse* 8.2 (1938): 32.

3. "Clark Street," *College Verse* 8.2 (1938): 32–33.

4. "This Was He," *College Verse* 8.2 (1938): 31.

5. Louise Bogan, "The Heart and the Lyre" in *A Poet's Alphabet: Reflections on the Literary Art and Vocation*, ed. Robert Phelps and Ruth Limmer (New York: McGraw, 1970), 429.

6. Cheryl Walker, *The Nightingale's Burden*, 47.

7. Suzanne Juhasz, *Naked and Fiery Forms: Modern American Poetry by Women, A New Tradition* (New York: Octagon, 1978), 1.

8. Jane Mayhall, "A Reckless Grandeur: The Poetry of Jean Garrigue," in *Ex Libris Jean Garrigue* (Saratoga Springs, N.Y.: Skidmore College Library, 1975) 21.

4. Water Walks and the Authority of Desire

1. Alicia Suskin Ostriker, *Stealing the Language: The Emergence of Women's Poetry in America* (Boston: Beacon, 1986), 110.

2. Jean Garrigue, "James Dickey: Airborne and Earthbound," *New Leader* 22 May (1967): 21–22.

3. Luce Irigaray, *This Sex Which Is Not One*, 117.

4. Alicia Ostriker, *Stealing the Language*, 109.

5. Jean Garrigue, "The Other One," *Cross-Section 1947*, ed. Edwin Seaver (New York: Simon, 1947), 509.

6. A. R. Ammons, "A Poem Is a Walk," in *Claims for Poetry*, ed. Donald Hall (Ann Arbor: University of Michigan Press, 1982), 5.

7. Ibid., 6.

8. Jean Garrigue, "A Consideration of Mr. Arcularis, the Play," *Wake* 11 (1952): 77.

9. Grace Schulman, "To Create the Self," *Twentieth-Century Literature* 23 (1977): 311.

10. Sandra M. Gilbert and Susan Gubar, *The Madwoman in the Attic: The Woman Writer and the Nineteenth-Century Literary Imagination* (New Haven: Yale University Press, 1979), 84.

11. Deborah Pope, *A Separate Vision: Isolation in Contemporary Women's Poetry* (Baton Rouge: Louisiana State University Press, 1984), 163.

12. Judith Fryer, *Felicitous Space: The Imaginative Structures of Edith Wharton and Willa Cather* (Chapel Hill: University of North Carolina Press, 1986), 49–50.

Postscript

1. Jean Garrigue, "Doggerel of a Diehard Who Sleeps in a Nest of Newspapers," *From Deborah and Sappho to the Present: An Anthology of Women Poets*, vol. 4, ed. Mildred Wiackley (New York: New Orlando, 1976) 97–99. The poem was first published in the *Kenyon Review* 25 (1963): 125–28. I have chosen to quote from Garrigue's later version.

2. See Jean Garrigue's "For an Orchard Tree," *Literary Review* 5 (1961): 87–89.

INDEX